BLESSED, BLESSED . . . BLESSED

The Untold Story of Our Family's Fight to
Love Hard, Stay Strong, and Keep the Faith
When Life Can't Be Fixed

BLESSED, BLESSED...
BLESSED

MISSY
ROBERTSON
with Beth Clark

TYNDALE®
MOMENTUM

An Imprint of
Tyndale House Publishers, Inc.

Library of Congress Cataloging-in-Publication Data

Robertson, Missy, date.
 Blessed, blessed. . . blessed : the untold story of our family's fight to love hard, stay strong, and keep the faith when life can't be fixed / Missy Robertson, with Beth Clark.
  pages cm
 Includes bibliographical references.
 ISBN 978-1-4964-0570-8 (hc)
 1. Suffering—Religious aspects—Christianity. 2. Families—Religious life. 3. Cleft palate—Religious aspects—Christianity. I. Title.
  BV4909.R635 2015
  248.8'60922—dc23
  [B]   2015024106

Printed in the United States of America

21	20	19	18	17	16	15
7	6	5	4	3	2	1

To my children—Reed, Cole, and Mia.

*May the words in this book cause you to realize
how extraordinarily well you have handled such
traumatic life situations, even though, to you,
each circumstance was just part of normal life.
May they also help you to grasp a glimpse into just
how much your dad and I love you and would go
to the ends of the earth for you.*

Table of Contents

Foreword

SHORTLY AFTER MY EIGHTEENTH BIRTHDAY, I made a declaration that I would be a single man for the rest of my life. That was it! No more dating for me. The vow of lifelong celibacy was in response to my latest dating relationship gone awry. A few days later, I picked up Missy at her house so we could attend a football game at her high school. We didn't view this as a "date" since we had both recently gotten out of relationships. I decided to make an exception to my new vow because I knew she was a young woman of faith in God, and her stunning beauty was impossible to overlook. She quickly became my best friend, and nearly three years later she would become my wife and lifelong partner.

I was so happy when she actually said "I do." Despite our physical attraction to each other while we were engaged, we decided to focus our relationship on our mutual faith in God and remain pure until marriage. The spiritual foundation we laid for our life together was based on love, joy, peace, patience, kindness, goodness, faithfulness, gentleness, and self-control. These qualities are known as the fruit of the Holy Spirit, who we believe exists in our hearts.

Since we'd waited, our wedding night was all the sweeter. Missy and I decided to wait a while before we had kids so we could continue building a strong foundation for our future family. Being together made us both happy—or as my dad would say, "happy, happy, happy." That's happiness with a double dose of validation.

In our nearly twenty-five years of marriage, we have been blessed, blessed . . . blessed with three wonderful kids who we believe are gifts from God. To me, the meaning of the word *blessed* is similar to the definition of happiness but goes even deeper, reflecting a joy that comes from a divine origin. There are times when blessings from God are difficult to recognize because we cannot see the world through God's eyes, and we're unable to understand all of His ways. But God asks us to remain faithful to Him and wait until the blessing becomes apparent. Missy and I are not ashamed of our faith in God and welcome every opportunity to share it with others.

The two of us were thrilled when our two sons—Reed and Cole—were born. And then came our daughter, Mia. From the time we could see her in Missy's womb, we knew her life would be filled with special challenges. I vividly remember how she struggled to breathe when she was born. When she was being whisked away to intensive care, my first thought was, *Please, God, let her live!* And she did! That day I made a promise to Mia in my heart that I was going to help her in every way possible.

For the most part, this book is about the dot, dot, dot in *Blessed, Blessed . . . Blessed.* Missy has been an incredible mother during Mia's journey and has helped me deal with the "new normal" in our family multiple times throughout this difficult process. Missy is the most qualified person I know to recount Mia's courageous marathon with her cleft lip and palate because Missy has been just as brave throughout this ordeal.

People often ask me, "How's Mia?" I usually answer "good" no matter what procedure she is facing, but in my mind I'm thinking, *It's complicated!* Most people think that cleft lip and palate is merely a cosmetic issue that can be quickly fixed. In fact, that was my initial mind-set too, thinking, *My daughter has a problem. Let's fix it and move on.* If only it could be that simple. The harsh reality is that kids like Mia have surgeries and procedures to aid their speech, eating, and breathing the entire time they are growing. In severe cases, where there is no medical care available, a person could have difficulty speaking and extreme discomfort when trying to eat or breathe; in some instances, it could be life threatening. I'll admit that a general lack of understanding about Mia's condition has generated comments that can be frustrating. However, being from a family of talkers and ramblers, I am used to hearing a few dumb statements made with the best intentions, coming from sincere people.

We are extremely grateful that Mia's condition is being managed by some of the most talented doctors in the world. I've observed the compassion of these professionals who attend to cosmetic needs while also relieving suffering—giving kids reasons to smile and in some cases saving lives. We have been blessed by the encouragement of our family, friends, and the expertise of Mia's medical team.

Most important, our family believes that God doesn't make mistakes. He determines each and every detail of our lives. There is an interesting story in the Bible in John 9. Jesus and his disciples are walking together and encounter a man who was born blind. The disciples ask Jesus, "Rabbi, who sinned, this man or his parents, that he was born blind?" (verse 2). "Neither this man nor his parents sinned," said Jesus, "but *this happened so that the works of God might be displayed* in him" (verse 3, emphasis added). I know that "the works of God" are being displayed in Mia's life and are impacting people every day.

There is always a spiritual response to the things that happen to us physically. Jesus offers a new normal, if we have accepted Him, through His grace. A transformation occurs from the inside out through the Holy Spirit.

As the years have gone by, I've realized how Mia has helped me to grow spiritually. I have seen firsthand how she lives out Romans 5:3-5. The physical suffering Mia has experienced has produced in her incredible perseverance, character, and hope.

In Romans 5:6-8, the apostle Paul reveals the person who has suffered the most for all of us—Jesus Christ. "While we were still sinners, Christ *died* for us" (verse 8, emphasis added). It is the ultimate expression of God's love, a gift freely offered to you and to me.

Mia has handled her challenges much better than the rest of us. I believe it is difficult to live with circumstances that you have very little control over, but she seems to do it with lots of laughs and a zesty personality that people are drawn to. When innocent people suffer, it motivates the rest of us to stop complaining and start living unselfishly. Those who display courage inspire us to live life to the fullest. May you be encouraged through Mia's journey.

Thank you, Missy, for all you do for our family and also for writing this book. Without you I could not be me—but God knew that, didn't He?

I love you.

Jase

Introduction

I GREW UP WANTING to make a difference for God. For as long as I can remember, something inside of me has longed for Him to use me in a significant way. For many years, it didn't seem like it would happen. Then, in a completely unexpected turn of events, two situations began to weave themselves into everything else in my life. God orchestrated and combined those two things in a way that has given my husband, Jase, and me a platform and a level of visibility in the public eye we never, *ever* imagined we would have. Not in our wildest dreams.

The first event happened in the summer of 2003. I was pregnant and scheduled for an ultrasound at thirty-one weeks. It was truly a family affair, with our two young sons, Reed and Cole; my mother-in-law, best known as "Miss Kay" Robertson from the television show *Duck Dynasty*; and my sisters-in-law Lisa and Jessica with me. Jase wasn't there in person, but I knew he was there in spirit and would share in the excitement later when he saw the video.

We were all eager to see the new baby in amazing detail on the monitor, but a few minutes into the procedure, the ultrasound technician's expression signaled that there was a serious problem. She was a friend, and I knew her well enough to read the look of concern and sadness on her face. When she left to find the doctor, Miss Kay quickly whisked Reed and Cole out of the room.

Minutes later, when the doctor came in and checked the ultrasound, she broke the news that our unborn daughter had a cleft lip. I knew that was not good, but I did not realize how that one moment would put me and my family on a journey we had never imagined. A journey of faith, a journey of prayer, a journey that has sometimes been anxious, stressful, and painful, but one that has strengthened us and taught us lessons we never would have known without it.

Jase and I had already been blessed with two healthy boys without special needs, but there wasn't any doubt that Mia was a blessing, too, even when we learned that her condition was more complex than what was originally seen in the ultrasound. Yes, we were truly blessed, blessed . . . blessed with three children, each of them a unique gift to us from God.

Mia's condition has allowed us access to a community of people dealing with childhood medical challenges, a whole new world we never before knew existed, but one we are glad God allowed us to discover. We have met some of the most amazing people, especially patients and families also dealing with cleft. At times, those people have been lifelines and support systems for us, and at other times, we have been able to provide them with the resources and encouragement they need.

And personally, for Jase and me, we have learned to understand each other and work together as husband and wife in ways many couples never have to think about. That is a blessing all its own, adding to the deep level of power and strength shown to us by extended family and Christian friends.

If all we experienced were the many people we have met as a

result of Mia's journey and the relationships we have developed along the way, we certainly would have felt blessed. That would have been enough. But God had more than that in mind. Back in the day, we would have laughed our heads off over the idea that our family would ever be on television, but God knew He would shine a spotlight on us, and one way Jase and I would use that visibility would be to bring attention to what Mia was going through. This way we could help other families walking the same journey that is now so familiar to us.

The second development that put me in the unexpected position to be used by God in the way I had longed for since childhood was *Duck Dynasty.* Trust me, I don't know if anyone in the Robertson family, except Jase's brother Willie, would ever have come up with the idea of putting our family on television. In our minds, we have always been normal people doing our best to love God, love each other, and raise our children well. Those commitments have shaped Jase's and my lives since we first met. Had we been able to do those three things in complete obscurity, we would have been perfectly happy.

When the idea of a television show surfaced, Jase and I viewed it as a chance to go public with our faith. We were not swept away by the ideas of fame and fortune. For us, fame never was important. And fortune? We were people who lived within our means already and practiced great discipline in our finances. By the time *Duck Dynasty* came along, we had lived frugally for years, and while the idea of having more money, and the freedom and opportunities that come with it, sounded nice, it was not something we got especially excited about. We were fine with or without a television show. We determined early on that we would not allow any of the trappings that come with being celebrities to change our values, shift our priorities, or cause us to try to become people we are not. We knew we would find certain things easier to do once our level of income increased, and that has been true. But overall, I think anyone who knew Jase and me fifteen years ago would quickly say that the essence of who we are and the fundamentals of what we believe have not changed.

Aside from being a lot of fun and providing amazing opportunities for our family, *Duck Dynasty* has given Jase and me public personas we would never have had without a television show, allowing us to raise awareness of Mia's condition and how much it affects others. We can empathize with anyone who is struggling with a medical situation, or any kind of significant challenge, to help them put everything in perspective.

Many times, parents find a childhood medical condition completely overwhelming. Almost before they know it, that illness or injury can take over the parents' marriage and the life of the entire family. When this happens, everyone suffers.

One reason I wanted to write this book is to help families navigate through their difficulties, rather than having the challenges take charge and rule the family. Another reason I wanted to share our story is to encourage people facing any type of trouble in life that there is always hope, that the burden you think you can't bear is already in God's hands.

As any reader will see in the following pages, Jase and I have endured more sadness and difficulty than many people realize. Through every circumstance, we have leaned on our faith, and we have found God to be completely trustworthy and faithful. We know what it's like to hear bad news. We know how it feels to pray that God will do one thing in a situation, only to realize He has done something else. We know how easily each member of a family can be thrown off balance by one person's challenges, and we are well acquainted with the financial strain of a major medical situation.

Whether you find yourself reading this book out of curiosity because you are a fan of our show, out of desperation because you, too, have a child with special needs, or for some reason in between, I'm glad you picked it up. I hope our story will strengthen your faith, encourage you to keep trusting God with your impossible burden no matter how bleak things appear, and remind you that prayer really does make a difference. I have made every effort to tell our story with as much transparency and honesty as possible. You'll quickly see that everything has not been easy for us, as I'm sure it has not been easy for you. But in the end, as you walk with God, I pray that despite the challenges you face, you will view your life as I view mine: *blessed.*

I

Blessed Beginnings

THE ULTRASOUND ROOM was abuzz with happy anticipation as the technician, a former coworker of mine, prepared for the scan. As the image of our daughter's face became clear on the screen, we were ooh-ing and aah-ing and commenting on how cute her little cheeks were. Then the adults in the room grew quiet.

"Does her nose look smushed to you?" I asked the technician.

She simply said, "I need to get the doctor."

This wouldn't be the first and only time that we would be seeing doctors on Mia's behalf. Little did Jase and I know that a whole new chapter of our lives was about to unfold. Thankfully, we had come a long way from our very start, a memorable Christmas in 1988.

∽

I did not have to say a word.

The look on my face communicated everything to Jase Robertson when he presented me with my Christmas gift in 1988. It was a potted plant, not even a very big one or some exotic species, just an ordinary plant in a plain clay pot. Since I could not hide my confusion, I stared at him with a look that clearly said, "Are you *kidding* me?"

Sensing that I was not exactly pleased with this present, Jase could hardly restrain himself from grinning as he told me to "dig around in the dirt." As I dug, I found a small box covered in felt (and dirt). I knew immediately that it was a jewelry box but had no idea that the box held a beautiful engagement ring! Once again, the look on my face communicated everything I wanted to say, which was great, because I was so excited and surprised I could not speak.

Jase looked at me and proposed in his unique way, not gushing about how much he loved me and tenderly asking for my hand in marriage. He simply said with complete confidence, "Well, you're gonna marry me, aren't ya?"

Too thrilled and shocked to say very much, I managed to answer yes, and that was the beginning of a commitment the two of us still hold and treasure to this day, one that now includes our two amazing sons, Reed and Cole, and our remarkable daughter, Mia. We have a wonderful life together, but it did not just happen to us. Since the very beginning, when Jase and I first met, we have had challenges to overcome. We are still facing challenges, and with God's grace and help, we are still overcoming them.

Apples and Oranges

The differences between Jase and me were obvious from the start. For one thing, he had already graduated from high school by the time we met, while I still had two years left. Beyond that, our backgrounds had almost nothing in common, except that we were both committed Christians and had both been raised in West Monroe, Louisiana.

Jase was the second son born to Phil and Kay Robertson, whose tumultuous early years of marriage are well known. Jase grew up having to take care of himself in many ways or under the watchful eye and caring hand of his older brother, Alan. I was born in Lubbock, Texas, but my family moved to West Monroe when I was six months old. My father was a preacher, and my mother was a music teacher. My childhood was as stable and structured as Jase's was unsettled and unstructured.

By the time Jase's family got established in rural West Monroe after living in Arkansas and in a couple of small towns in Louisiana, he was surrounded by three brothers; a host of aunts, uncles, cousins; and his paternal grandparents, Granny and Pa, who lived in a little house on Phil and Miss Kay's property. The Robertsons were accustomed to big family meals, large holiday celebrations, and having lots of people around. Phil and Miss Kay have always had an open-door policy in their home, eager to feed someone, clothe someone, or give someone a place to sleep. Many times, Jase walked out of his bedroom to find a stranger sleeping on the sofa, and he hardly ever walked out his front door without running into a relative.

I, on the other hand, grew up with one brother, and with no grandparents, aunts, uncles, or cousins nearby. When we wanted to visit family, we had to travel out of town, which we could do only once or twice a year. My mother's parents often invited missionaries or traveling preachers to stay at their house, but my father's family kept to themselves and did not welcome outsiders into their home. When my parents married, they basically followed my paternal grandparents' example, and we rarely had guests for meals or an overnight visit.

Every Saturday, my brother and I helped our parents with household chores, such as dusting, vacuuming, and cleaning. My dad often said, "Cleanliness is next to godliness," and after meeting Jase, I quickly realized that the Robertson family did not regard this proverb as highly as my family did.

I remember one Saturday when Jase called me and asked if

we could go out that night. I told him I'd like to but I had to dust first.

"Dust?" he asked. "What does that mean?"

"You know, dust the furniture."

Silence.

"Like, take a rag, spray Pledge onto the furniture, and wipe it clean."

Yes, I actually had to explain to Jase that the word *dust* could be used as a verb as well as a noun.

Obviously, the Robertsons' open door and relaxed, unstructured ways were completely foreign to me, but I liked them.

I went to a private Christian school. Jase went to public school. As a teenager, I liked spending weekends with friends or going to ballgames. Jase wanted to spend his weekends outdoors and was happy as long as his activities included a fishing pole or a shotgun. My family bought ingredients for our meals at the grocery store. Jase's family had two primary ways of providing dinner for themselves: They either caught it or shot it, then skinned it and dressed it. My family lived in a well-kept house with a paved driveway in a suburban neighborhood. Jase's family lived in the country, and everyone parked their cars in the front yard.

When Jase and I first started dating, I had no idea how little crossover existed between the ways we grew up. All I knew was that he was very good looking, he was serious about his faith, and he had a self-possessed, self-confident quality that I had not seen in other guys. He was not interested in impressing anyone, including me. He was so comfortable and secure in who he was that I knew right away "what you see is what you get." He was determined to be true to God and true to himself. I understood that about him soon after we met, and I liked it.

Jase wanted to make sure I understood something else about him. When we reached a point in our relationship where we knew we could become serious about each other, he said to me, "You need to know something about me. I hunt *every day* of duck season. I will not give that up. Are you prepared for that?"

"Okay," I said. "If this relationship goes where I think it might go, I will not complain about your duck hunting every day of duck season. But in return, I want you to agree to send our children to OCS." OCS stands for Ouachita Christian School, the school I attended growing up. My parents had helped found the school, and my mother had taught music there. I had such a wonderful experience at that school, and being able to provide that same opportunity for my children was important to me. Jase agreed, so we had a deal.

I Had No Idea

Exactly what it means for a man to go duck hunting *every day* of the season may need some explanation. Duck season can last up to about three months, but it does not open and close on the same days every year. Some states also have a break in the season for about two weeks; that break is called "the split." When the split occurs in one state, ducks can still be hunted in other states. When Jase said he hunted every day of duck season, that meant he could be away from home for a couple of weeks at a time.

During duck season, his alarm clock goes off sometime between 3:00 and 4:00 every morning. He typically stays in the duck blind for hours—all day if necessary—to get the allowed limit of ducks per day. When we were dating, and for most of our marriage, the Robertsons' family business, Duck Commander, operated out of Phil and Kay's house, so Jase went there to make duck calls once he finished hunting. I hardly ever saw him during daylight hours.

I had to come to understand that while some people hunt for fun or recreation, Robertson men hunt for a living. Duck hunting is not a hobby in our family; it's a big part of our livelihood. For years, our family survived solely off the sales of the annual Duck Commander hunting videos. If the ducks were not flying over West Monroe, Phil and Jase had to find them somewhere else in order to make that video to support our families. The Robertsons hunted long before *Duck Dynasty* ever entered anyone's mind, and they will be hunting long after the show finishes its run. Hunting is not optional for Jase; it's part of who he is. Sometimes that means he operates without enough sleep. That wears on a person—and on his wife and family.

Phil and Jase hunt more than anyone else in the family and take hunting more seriously than the others, so Miss Kay totally understands how I feel once duck season starts. She has said more than once, "I sure hope I don't die during duck season because none of the men in the family would come to my funeral!" I have to say, she has good reason to be concerned.

One day during the early years of our marriage, before cell phones, Jase left for his usual day of hunting and filming with Phil. Our routine was that Jase would usually either call me when he got back to his parents' house or have Miss Kay call me to tell me he was on his way home. This communication became a lifeline for me—knowing that my husband was okay and that another day of duck season was behind us. On that particular day, Phil had returned home in the early afternoon without Jase, eaten lunch, and was taking his nap, which I learned when I talked to Miss Kay. She assured me she would call me when Jase arrived.

By late afternoon, I still had not heard from Jase. By evening, long after the sky was dark, and just as I was about to panic, the phone rang. Jase, acting completely relaxed and even jovial about his successful hunt that day, could not understand why I was almost hysterical with worry. He had been out there alone for hours! "Missy," he said calmly, "you need to understand something. I am more comfortable driving a boat at night, by myself, than I will ever be driving a car in the middle of the day down the interstate. You never need to worry about me when I'm out on the river. That's where I grew up." I have never forgotten that conversation, but I will admit I still worry every once in a while.

Since no one on my side of the family was a hunter, I did not fully understand what being married to a serious hunter would actually mean, but I know now. His early mornings and long absences are not my favorite things about being his wife, but he did try to warn me about the reality of this unusual vocation, so it's something I've grown used to.

Early in 1991, a few months into our marriage and soon after US troops were sent to Operation Desert Storm, I watched a national news story in which the wife of a serviceman was being interviewed. She described certain sacrifices that her family had to make because her husband was gone. She had to quit her job in order to take care of her small children (since she and her husband had shared that responsibility before he was deployed), and money was tight. When the journalist asked her how she was making ends meet, one of the examples she mentioned was that she washed and saved aluminum foil to be used multiple times. Reusing aluminum foil? I had never thought about doing that. Jase and I didn't have much money, but I didn't have to save aluminum foil!

That wife's story hit me hard as I listened to the entire news broadcast, and at the ripe old age of nineteen I began to comprehend how much our military families were sacrificing for us. Not only do they sacrifice financial stability; they also sacrifice their own safety when called on a mission, a mission that is on our behalf. They ensure that the *rest* of us keep our freedoms—including choosing an occupation such as hunting.

Many times when Jase is out of town for long periods of time, one of my married friends or acquaintances will snidely remark, "I don't know how you handle it. I would never let my husband do that." First of all, that's a decision Jase and I made together, long before we got married. Yes, it has been difficult at times, especially when the boys were little. But all I could think about when hearing those comments was, *At least he's not fighting in a war overseas! Those wives are the ones who have it hard. I don't know how they do it.* Whenever I am asked how I handle Jase being gone so much, I always think of that news story. At the risk of sounding boastful, I'll tell you that I handle it like a champ!

We Were Meant to Be

Once Jase knew I would not interfere with hunting season and I knew he would honor my desire to send our children to the school of my choice, we could move toward engagement and marriage. Despite our differences, we knew we were meant to be together. The commonalities of our faith and shared values forged a powerful bond between us, in addition to the elements of enjoying each other's company and the mutual attraction we could not deny.

By the time Jase and I became engaged, not only had we become best friends, but I also knew beyond any question that Jase was God's man for me, and I was God's woman for him—for the rest of our lives, no matter what. We married on August 10, 1990. Our wedding took place in the same church we still attend with many longtime friends and members of our extended family.

I was nineteen years old when we married, and Jase was six days from turning twenty-one. The day was everything I always dreamed it would be. I wore a beautiful wedding gown hand-made by my mother's best friend, a perfect duplicate of an expensive designer dress I had seen at a bridal store, down to its last tiny bits of beading, lacework, and tufts of tulle. As someone who has always loved music and enjoyed singing all my life, I wanted to be both the bride and the soloist at my wedding, so I prerecorded a song called "Only God Could Love You More" to be played as I walked down the aisle.

Jase and I made a deliberate decision while we were dating to remain sexually pure until we were married. Keeping that commitment was not easy, but we did it. We decided to trust God, and we were determined to honor His Word no matter how much of a struggle it was. The important thing is we made it! Two years, ten months, and two days, but who was counting? The first sexual experience either one of us ever had took place with each other on our wedding night. Jase often says it was more like an exploratory biological experiment! We have remained faithful to one another and our marriage vows since that day.

Thank You, Miss Kay and Lisa

Jase and I dated for almost three years before we married, long enough that I had the opportunity to spend a good bit of time around his family. The differences between the Robertsons and my family didn't faze me. I enjoyed visiting their home and realized before Jase and I married that Miss Kay could teach me a lot about being a wife to a Robertson man. I had seen the way she treated Phil—her attentiveness to his every need, her servant's heart toward him, and her overall affection for him.

I knew Miss Kay was Jase's role model for his future wife. He had certain expectations for the woman he planned to marry, and Miss Kay had set a high standard. Because I admired and respected her and also wanted to please my future husband, I was eager to learn the lessons she already knew. I was not trying to become a duplicate of Miss Kay; I knew I had to be true to myself, but I also saw the value in demonstrating toward my husband the attitudes and actions she used with hers. From Miss Kay, I learned partly by instruction, but mostly by example, how to love and honor my husband.

While Jase and I were dating, and during the first years of our marriage, Jase's older brother, Alan, and his wife, Lisa, also lived on Phil and Miss Kay's property with their two young daughters. I knew Lisa, the first Robertson daughter-in-law, would also help and support me. At that time I looked to Lisa as an ideal young wife and mother, the person I went to for advice on fitting into the family.

However, I was unaware of some of the things Lisa was struggling with personally at that time—emotional scars inflicted on her for years from an abusive male relative as well as sometimes feeling ignored by Alan because he spent so much time with his parents and brothers. While Alan was helping his dad in the struggling duck call business, Lisa worked hard to support their family.

As the difficulties in her marriage began to escalate, Lisa had an extramarital affair with a casual acquaintance, followed a few years later by a more serious affair with someone she had known in high school. While those things were happening, I felt abandoned and betrayed by someone I trusted. But Alan's forgiveness and reconciliation with Lisa restored their marriage, and over a period of time I regained my deep respect and love for her. Lisa demonstrated strength, courage, and humility once she decided to end her affairs, speak honestly about them, and embrace God's forgiveness.[1]

Due in part to Lisa's unfaithfulness to Alan, Jase developed some problems trusting me around other men and had bouts of jealousy that we had to work through for years in our marriage. It was very difficult at the time for him to see his brother so badly hurt. Over time, Alan and Lisa, along with others, helped us both with this issue. She quickly became the older sister I never had. Jase and I spent many nights at their house hanging out, watching television together, and playing with their sweet babies. Lisa was outspoken, funny, a great cook, and a woman deeply in love with her husband. These qualities were admirable to me.

When Jase and I were married, I didn't know how to cook. Growing up, my mother had always prepared meals for our family, but she did not enjoy cooking the way Miss Kay does. I knew that once we were married, Jase would expect the kinds of meals his mom prepared, so I asked her to teach me to cook. I am not sure she was prepared for how completely inexperienced I was. The only cooking endeavor I felt confident in at that point in my life was making a mean macaroni and cheese out of a box. She was definitely surprised by some of the things I did not know, such as how to tell when boiled potatoes were done. But once she realized I needed serious help, she was patient and kind as she helped me find my way around the kitchen.

We started with the basics: how to brown meat, how to mash potatoes, and even how to heat canned vegetables on the stove, which I had never done before. She also taught me how to plan a meal, including which starches go best with certain meats and how to make her famous homemade white sauce. Without her help, I would have been lost and frustrated in the kitchen, and Jase would have been hungry.

Since I had never lived alone before getting married (I mean, there wasn't really any time for that), I never *had* to learn how to cook or take care of myself. Besides, being raised in a structured environment, I ate only at breakfast time, lunchtime, and dinnertime. Period. Jase's family ate whenever they wanted to eat. If that meant frying fish at 10:30 in the morning because Phil just caught it and was "fish hungry," then that's when they ate it. They even had pancakes and bacon for supper sometimes. I had never heard of such a thing! I grew up in a family that ate to live, but married into a family that lived to eat. Talk about a contrast.

Another way I wanted to please Jase was to make a comfortable home for him. Since neither of us nor our families had any money, almost every piece of furniture we had was a hand-me-down from a family member. We had a desk and a chair from Granny and Pa, along with a sectional couch and a water bed (yes, we had a water bed) handed down from my aunt Bonny. I bought a table and chairs for fifty dollars at a garage sale. Someone gave us an entertainment center that they were going to throw out, and my grandparents bought us a nineteen-inch television as a wedding present. But I made it all work. I decorated the living room with throw pillows that had ducks on them, framed prints of ducks, and laid out duck knickknacks. It was perfect!

Loving and Serving in the Early Years

One of the things Jase and I looked forward to before we married was being able to use our home for ministry—Bible teaching, encouragement, and Christian fellowship—as I had seen take place at Miss Kay and Phil's house. We hoped that one day, when we had a home big enough to handle it, we could open our doors the way they did. That dream became a reality, in a much bigger way than we ever expected, about two weeks after our wedding.

A week after returning from our honeymoon, Jase baptized his best friend—then another friend, then a friend's girlfriend. All of these people wanted to know more about God, so Jase and I began teaching them. The more we shared our faith, the more people crowded into our tiny apartment, and more and more of our time away from work became focused on ministering to others. What I assumed would be cozy evenings at home with my new husband ended up being busy nights with many troubled young people searching for purpose in life.

By the end of our first year of marriage, we had baptized more than a hundred people. Many of those new believers not only needed counseling, help with studying the Bible, and straightforward biblical teaching, but they also needed somewhere to go every night to keep themselves out of trouble, all of which Jase and I were happy to provide—well, most of the time. I knew we were doing what God wanted us to do, but I longed for the moments when Jase and I could be alone. This was definitely a challenging time for our marriage, but we journeyed on.

At first, I felt overwhelmed and inadequate to teach God's Word or share devotional thoughts with others. I had been raised in a pretty sheltered environment and was not nearly as experienced in the ways of the world as some of the people who came to me for direction in their Christian lives. I had never been drunk, had not had sex before marriage, and had never even contemplated trying drugs of any kind. I was naive to say the least. Most of the people who crowded our living room came from broken homes, had been physically or sexually abused, or had chosen a lifestyle of wild living and had hit their breaking point.

Jase tried to convince me that God would not have sent us people we could not help, and that we simply needed to do our best and let Him work through us. He also taught me how to have a poker face when I heard about certain things people had done, as I was shocked at some of the lifestyles I was learning about and realized I couldn't show it. These people were ashamed of their deeds and were seeking a way out of their lifestyles, willing to lay it all out on the table. They didn't need judgment from me; they needed reassurance that they could move past it all with the help of Jesus.

When we moved into our apartment as newlyweds, we never imagined it would become a wedding chapel. Several young couples who came to our Bible studies surrendered their lives to Christ and decided to marry. The problem was, most of them had been sexually active for months or years. After they became Christians, we encouraged them to stay pure until marriage. Understandably, they were not interested in long engagements and some of them wanted to marry on very short notice. As it turned out, they asked Jase, who had the legal authority, to preside.

One couple's wedding was scheduled for a Saturday night, but they showed up at our apartment on Tuesday and said they simply could not wait any longer. They told us that they were trying their best to stay sexually pure, but since they had never refrained from having sex in prior relationships, it was proving extremely difficult for them. I was so impressed with their new commitment to God and their willingness to live for Him. Jase performed an impromptu ceremony that night, and with the marriage license signed and in hand, their car squealed out of the apartment complex a few minutes later. The four of us kept their marriage a secret, even during their big wedding the following Saturday night. I often said to Jase after our apartment cleared out at night, "Boy, if these walls could talk."

To say that our first five years together were intensely devoted to ministry is not an understatement. At one point, we had groups in our home every night of the week, and that went on for months. We thrived on knowing that every day of our lives was filled with spiritual purpose, but there came a point when we knew we were ready for more.

"I'm Never Having Kids"

As Jase and I began to prepare to start a family, I had to give myself credit for coming a long way in my thoughts about motherhood. I knew I wanted two boys and a girl, a big change from my younger days, when I did not want children at all. I distinctly remember the announcement I made to my parents when I was eleven or twelve years old: "I'm never having kids."

Let me explain. My father was a pastor; I went to church every time the doors were open, and I paid attention to the Sunday school lessons and the preaching I heard each week. In addition, I knew my Bible well as a preteen, and the Bible said having children was painful. My decision not to become a mother had little to do with raising children; it had everything to do with the pain of giving birth to them, pain of biblical proportions! I knew that I was *not* interested in that.

When the subject came up one day while we were riding in the car, my dad said, "They give you pain medicine so it won't hurt." That information was not especially helpful because once I found out the pain medicine had to be injected, I did not want that either. I was terrified of being stuck with needles! Since I was a healthy child who rarely had to see the doctor except for annual checkups, getting a shot was a very big deal.

I loved babies and children and enjoyed babysitting every time I had the chance. In my heart, I had always wanted to raise children. *Maybe adoption is the answer,* I thought. After a little more time passed, I decided that after I got married one pregnancy might be okay—as long as I had twins so I could get everything over and done with.

But as is the case with so many young women, after I became the wife of a wonderful man, I found myself longing for a baby and wanting to become a mother. This came as no surprise to my parents. They always knew I would grow out of my adolescent declarations and change my mind once I settled down with the right person. They were right.

After Jase and I married, we decided not to start a family right away. We wanted to wait a few years, giving ourselves time to establish a firm foundation for our marriage and our relationship with each other. We wanted to prepare ourselves as best we could for parenthood before bringing a baby into the world. Besides that, we realized how young we were and knew that once we started having children, our lives would change forever. We also were enjoying being very social and active with our friends. Jase played on city-league and church-league softball teams, which took us to the ballpark about four nights a week in the spring and summer. I was involved in church musicals and singing on the praise team, as well as keeping house for what seemed like round-the-clock game nights, Bible studies, and movie marathons.

While the nights were a lot of fun, cleaning up after twenty to fifty people the following mornings before leaving for work was definitely not something I had envisioned as a dreamy-eyed girl planning out my marriage. Sometimes I had to put a handwritten sign on our door stating "This house is closed to guests until to-morrow" or "We're having family time." The first time I posted the sign, I actually had someone ask me the next evening exactly what "family time" meant, and how we could have family time when we didn't have children yet?

Well, Jase and I thought, *maybe we should do something about that.*

I have always been the kind of person who wants to know as much as possible about anything in which I am involved. If I know I am going to face an unfamiliar situation, especially something I have heard can be challenging, I believe knowledge is one of the best tools I can have. No matter how much time or energy I have to invest, I will read, study, talk to people, and do any other research necessary to equip myself for new circumstances in life. This aspect of my personality served me well as Jase and I began thinking about having children. Our church held several classes on family relationships and parenting, and I went to as many as I possibly could.

I continued attending classes after I became pregnant with our first child in 1994. During one of the meetings, a woman I still greatly admire to this day made a comment I will never forget. She said, "The best gift you can give your children is to love your husband." Since the moment I heard those words, I have tried to live up to them because I am so convinced they are true.

As of this writing, Jase and I have been married twenty-five years. I cannot imagine a better husband, a better father for our children, or a better leader for our family. Talk about being blessed! The path we travel in our life together is not always easy, but I would not want to walk it with anyone else.

2

"Of Course I'm Having Kids!"

OUR FIRST SON, Reed Silas Robertson, decided to test my resolve to have children by delaying his arrival. My due date was May 5, 1995, and my obstetrician was scheduled to leave on vacation shortly after. She was one of ten doctors I worked for as an administrative assistant at a local obstetrics and gynecology (ob-gyn) clinic, so I knew her as both my doctor and one of my employers. If Reed wasn't born on his due date or hadn't come while she was away, I was scheduled to meet her at the hospital on May 15 for labor to be induced.

At 6 a.m. on May 15, Jase and I showed up at the hospital. It was the day after Mother's Day. The fears that had once made me declare, "I am never having kids" surfaced again. I was afraid of the pain. As it turned out, I had good reason to be afraid. Reed's birth was far from simple. On a scale of one to ten, my pain registered at seventy-five!

For the next several hours, nothing seemed to move very quickly. At 3:30 in the afternoon, the doctor broke my water, and by 5 p.m. I was dilated to three centimeters. For the next several minutes, I could hardly believe the pain, screaming silently inside, *I can't handle this!* Not only was I hurting physically, I felt guilty and ashamed for not being stronger. Angry and disappointed with myself, I struggled to breathe and wanted to cry. Without the benefit of my breathing techniques to control the pain, I told Jase to ask the nurse to order an epidural.

The nurse came in, rolled her eyes at me, and said, "The doctor said I could check you. If you're close to four centimeters, I'll go ahead and order it." I have never prayed so hard for the number four in all of my life!

I was in excruciating pain between 5:00 and 5:25 p.m. for good reason. Within a span of twenty-five minutes, I dilated from three centimeters to nine centimeters. I still wonder if that was some kind of record!

The nurse was as shocked as Jase and I were. In fact, she panicked, and that really upset me. I could see my stomach convulsing. When she gasped and said, "You're nine! It's too late for an epidural!" I cratered emotionally. My plans of a pain-free delivery were fading quickly.

Even though I was a wreck, I maintained my budget-mindedness. Loudly and emphatically, I said, "I *paid* for that epidural!" For the next two hours, with no medication whatsoever, I pushed. I kept pushing with no results because Reed had turned and was stuck in my pelvis—positioned so his face was facing my abdomen. Usually, the baby is facing the mother's back.

Meanwhile, my dad was outside of the delivery room with a 1990s-size video camera rolling. He has more than two hours of footage of a wooden door! A large crowd had gathered beside him and my mom outside the door—friends and family representing both sides were there. Reed would be the first grandchild on my side of the family and the first grandson on the Robertson side of the family, so there was lots of anticipation about seeing this baby. The Robertsons alone make up a sizable group of people, and the hospital stretched the rules, allowing them and everyone else to congregate outside my door. They had to be very quiet, because they really were not supposed to congregate in the hallway. The only reason they were allowed to be there is that the doctor had made an exception for me because of my working relationship with her.

After a lot of pushing with no progress, the nurse climbed onto the table and tried to push Reed out of my body. She put both of her hands on the top of my stomach and pushed downward, as though she were trying to push Reed down the birth canal. After I screamed, "No!" the doctor looked at the nurse and shook her head as if to say, "Don't do that again." When I screamed, "No!" I meant it, but I immediately felt bad and apologized to her, all during a contraction. My exclamation is actually one of the few sounds that can be heard on the video. Looking back, I don't think a scream was inappropriate at all.

Finally, the doctor decided a forceps delivery was necessary and ordered anesthesia. Then, in a move that shocked, hurt, and offended me, she turned her chair around, with her back to me, and started watching television. When Jase saw this scenario being played out, he realized that I could not choose to suddenly take a break. He knew I needed support, and once the next contraction started, he and the nurse jumped in to help me—encouraging me, telling me to push, reminding me that I could do it. In my mind, I knew there was nothing I could do but wait on the anesthesiologist, but my body never got that message. While the doctor watched television, my body kept trying to get the baby out. I knew my doctor couldn't do anything more until the anesthesiologist arrived, but I was appalled that she seemed to ignore me while I was suffering and struggling so intensely. After all, I was still having contractions every minute or so. Even a little false hope would have been appreciated at that point.

Gritting my teeth, I had a moment of déjà vu, remembering all the times I had watched television shows where women were in labor and dramatically crying out, "I can't do this!" I used to make fun of those scenes, saying, "That's so ridiculous. What are they going to do, live with a baby in their belly for the rest of their lives? What a silly thing to write into a script." Turns out, it wasn't so silly after all.

My body was still seizing in pain, and I felt complete despair. I wanted to give up. I looked at Jase and quietly said to him, "I can't do this." Jase, calm and collected as usual, stroked my head, looked at me with somewhat of a smirk, and said, "Yes, you can." Somehow, I believed him.

Once the anesthesiologist arrived, the nurse said to me, "This is the last contraction you'll ever feel." I sat through six more contractions as he attempted to find the right place to insert the needle. I had to sit upright on the edge of the table, with a baby almost-but-not-quite out of me. With blood dripping down my back, my muscles seized, and Jase dug his hands into my back trying to help. But not much was going to help me in any significant way except getting that baby out. Using the forceps, the doctor eventually delivered our healthy firstborn boy, Reed.

A few minutes later, Jase looked at Reed's cone-shaped head and said sincerely, "We'll still love him." I had to give him a break; this was his first child, and he had no idea that Reed's head would eventually look normal. He thought Reed would be cone-headed for the rest of his life! I'm sure one of our moms enlightened him fairly quickly, and they all had a good laugh about it.

As soon as the nurse handed our newborn to me, I felt an overwhelming connection to him, a bond I cannot describe, but one that other mothers understand. I thought he was the most incredible thing I had ever seen. In a moment I will never forget, I took Reed in my arms for the first time, and he turned his head all the way around to face me and looked straight into my eyes. I could hardly believe this baby, only a few minutes old, who had never seen a face before, found mine. I still wonder how he knew to look into my eyes, and after all these years, that powerful communication between mother and newborn still amazes me.

Finally, the door of my room was opened, and Jase took Reed out to meet our family and friends. I could hear everyone excitedly talking, relieved that our baby had finally arrived. After Jase handed Reed back to the nurses, he came back into the delivery room and held my hand while the nurses stitched and cleaned me. I must have fallen asleep because I don't remember much about that time. Jase later told me that he felt like he had been part of an R-rated horror movie because of the blood, pain, and graphic nature of this birthing experience, not to mention the occasional screams (mine, not his).

When the staff got ready to roll me back to my hospital room from the delivery room, I was completely exhausted beyond anything I had ever felt—mentally and physically. I remember very little about those moments except that I realized I was too tired to even open my eyes. All I remember hearing was the sound of Willie's voice cracking jokes and a comment that Reed's head was 14.5 inches in diameter. No wonder he had gotten stuck.

I was so totally spent that when the nurse asked me if I wanted her to bring Reed back so I could hold him, I said, "I cannot even open my eyes. I just can't take him right now." People have asked me if being unable to open my eyes had anything to do with the medication. It did not; I was *that* exhausted. The nurses let me rest all night and brought Reed to me the next morning.

A Robertson Through and Through

Like most expectant parents during the weeks and months before a baby's birth, Jase and I had many conversations about what to name our child. Jase wanted to name him Cypress Creek Robertson, with the nickname "Cy." He thought this was brilliant because his family lived on Cypress Creek, a small tributary off the Ouachita River. I immediately vetoed that idea.

At that point in time, I had not met Jase's favorite uncle, Si Robertson. I'm sure some people would even contend that he is now America's favorite TV uncle, but I knew very little about Si when Reed was born because he had been serving in the military for more than twenty-four years and had never lived in West Monroe. I simply knew that Jase was named after him—Jason Silas Robertson—and once I nixed "Cypress Creek," Jase wanted to name our firstborn son after Uncle Si too. Since his uncle's nickname "Si" is pronounced "Cy," Jase said, "That's the brilliant part of the plan!"

I said, "If we're gonna name him after you and your uncle, let's do it."

We also liked the name Reed, which has special meaning to us because Jase is one of the best duck call makers in the world. His ear is amazing, and he can duplicate the sound of many types of ducks to near perfection. One of the keys to his skill with duck calls is his remarkable ability to craft their reeds. Reed's name not only honors his great-uncle Si, it also honors his father's expertise.

Even though Jase and I had intentionally waited for almost five years to have a child, knowing it would change our lives, we had no idea how much change would occur. Having Reed didn't just change our lives; it turned them upside down. We went from our simple existence of doing almost anything we wanted to do at any time to being responsible for another living, breathing human being. This little person could not do anything for himself, and that was something I had to get used to—much more than I ever anticipated.

Since the day he was born, Reed has been a strong type A personality. He is always ready to go and always eager to speak his mind. He is not intimidated by conflict and is the kind of person who will argue simply to prove a point. (Hmm, sounds like a few more Robertsons I know.) The more heated a conversation becomes, the more he enjoys it. He does not necessarily love to argue for the sake of disagreeing with someone as much as he refuses to refrain from arguing if a disagreement is necessary to win his case. He is also one to test every boundary presented to him, making sure his daddy and I mean what we say. This is where consistency was born in my parenting skills!

When Reed was two years and ten months old, I decided it was high time for him to be potty trained. I had read a few books on how to accomplish this task, and most of the advice suggested a long, drawn-out process over a few weeks. Because I worked outside the home, and we had had another young child by that time, I chose to try to hit this process head-on and finish it quickly. So after Reed's nap one Thursday afternoon, I said to him, "You're a big boy now. You're not going to wear diapers anymore. You're going to start tee-teeing in the potty."

He immediately started screaming and crying, "I don't want to!"

I knew right then and there that he was ready.

For the next few hours, I left his bottoms off and asked him the same question, literally, every five minutes: "Do you need to tee-tee?"

Every single time I asked, his answer was the same: "No."

That evening, while I was in the kitchen cooking dinner, he walked toward me and stopped, saying nothing, but looking straight at me.

"Do you need to tee-tee?" I asked again.

He didn't answer. He simply glared at me with a glare I knew all too well. I knew what he was thinking.

"Don't do it," I said calmly.

The glare continued.

"Don't even think about it," I said sternly.

Without taking his eyes off of me for even a split second, he peed right there on my ceramic tile floor. By this point I knew the difference between his being defiant and having an accident. I immediately disciplined him strongly, and he understood that I would not give in to his silent, passive tantrum. He knew his days of wearing diapers were over. I reinforced that if he ever did anything like that again, he would receive the same punishment.

After that incident, he was very cooperative with the potty-training process, and by the time Sunday morning rolled around, he was wearing big boy underwear under his church clothes and doing great.

Reed is a born competitor, and whether he is on the football field or in the kitchen trying to convince me to give him permission to do something, he goes for the win, no matter what it takes. He is quite an artist, both on paper and in music, wowing us constantly with his talent. He refuses to take no for an answer, determined to make his dreams come true. He has grown into a God-fearing, fun-loving, determined young man, and we couldn't be more proud of him.

Another Adventurous Birth

A couple of years after Reed was born, the trauma surrounding his birth could not keep Jase and me from wanting another baby. I mean, my body was stretched as wide as humanly possible when he was born, so the next one should slide out quickly, right? We were so excited to be expecting a new baby on Christmas Eve of 1997, hoping and praying for a smooth pregnancy and a normal delivery with a lot less drama and a lot less pain than what surrounded Reed's birth. It did not exactly work out that way.

The first unusual situation we faced was that I started bleeding several weeks into my pregnancy. The doctor ordered an ultrasound and to our great relief said, "The baby's fine. Everything is okay." However, she went on to say, "You're sloughing off something, though. It looks like there was another baby." She finally concluded two embryos had been conceived and that they were growing in separate sacs. The doctor told me that it was a common occurrence under these circumstances for one of the babies not to be viable. In all of my prenatal visits prior to that day, she had only heard one heartbeat, so even though I was surprised and a little saddened by the news, I took it calmly. Jase and I were excited about the one baby we knew we were expecting and that the embryo was still safe, sound, and growing.

Several weeks before Cole's due date, the doctor told us he was breech. She explained my two options: She could manually turn him inside of me so his head would emerge first during a natural birth, or I could have a C-section. For several reasons, the idea of turning him was not appealing to me. First, even though I endured almost unbearable pain with Reed, I still wanted to avoid as much pain as possible—and turning my second baby sounded like an excruciating process. Second, I knew God had designed babies to position themselves for labor and delivery, and I felt there had to be a reason he was not headed in the right direction. I kept thinking, *We just don't need to mess with this by turning him.* Even though I did not want to have a major surgery so close to Christmas, I never was at peace with the idea of repositioning him, so I chose to have a C-section.

I scheduled the C-section for December 11, knowing I would need a couple of weeks to recover before Christmas, especially with busy, excited two-year-old Reed in the house, and because this was during our duck season split. Jase jokingly said the timing would be perfect since he would not be in the duck blind. Jase and I completed the necessary paperwork immediately after Thanksgiving and started our last-minute preparations for Cole's arrival. Despite Cole being breech, our plans were falling into place.

On the morning of December 4, something did not feel quite right. Since I never went into labor with Reed, I had no idea what labor felt like. When I had the same sensation several times, I decided to watch the clock. It was happening every eight minutes. I got Reed up and dressed, and we headed to my parents' house. I was going to drop him off with my mom before heading to work, as I did every morning, though by that point I was only working part-time.

"I don't know if this is important or not, but I'm feeling something every eight minutes," I told her.

"You're in labor!" she gasped excitedly.

The contractions were not very strong, but at my mother's insistence, I called my doctor. Her staff told me to go to the hospital and be placed on a monitor. If anything was happening, they said, the hospital would let the doctor know. So I drove myself to the hospital and checked in alone because it was December—duck hunting season. Jase was quite a distance away, and in those days when cell phones were not as widely used as they are now, I had no way to reach him. Thankfully my mom was pretty sure I was in labor, so she found a trusted friend to watch Reed and then joined me at the hospital.

Soon after I arrived at the hospital, I called Miss Kay to tell her I might be in labor. She was surprised, of course, and said, "Jase is out in the duck blind with Phil. I don't know how in the world we can get a message to him."

More than anything, I wanted Jase there, but I kept relatively calm because I was hooked up to a monitor that was supposed to register each contraction with a line that moved up and down, like a graph. It did not display any labor activity. I felt I might really be in labor, but I supposed the monitor knew best. *Not really.* The leads on the monitor were not attached properly, which is why it registered nothing. When the nurse applied them correctly, it showed I was in strong labor.

"We need to get you into the delivery room right now," the nurse told me.

No! I thought. *My husband is in a duck blind, and we have no way to reach him!* I immediately started crying, thinking, *I cannot even imagine doing this without Jase.* Crying did not help matters, as many pregnant women know that sinuses are not their friend during pregnancy, especially in the middle of winter. Even though I tried my hardest to hide my tears, my nose quickly stuffed up, and I had a hard time breathing.

In the midst of all the emotion, a nurse came into my room and said the hospital did not have any of my paperwork. With tears dotting the release forms, I re-signed all the papers. In the background, I heard the anesthesiologist say, "If we could get her to stop crying . . . ," but I couldn't. All I could think of was how much I wanted Jase there at that moment. In fact, I didn't think I could go through with the surgery without him, and I didn't even want to try. But there was no way he could get to the hospital in time.

I called Miss Kay again and gave her an update. She could hear the emotion in my voice and said sympathetically, "I can't get to him."

I was devastated.

I had no choice but to garner my courage to go through the C-section without my husband. I tried to be strong, but the words "He's not going to make it" kept assaulting my mind. As much as I wanted to keep my composure and as hard as I tried, I struggled terribly.

I do not remember anything about being prepared for surgery, but I do remember lying on the operating table. Because of my job at the clinic, I knew most of the nurses in the operating room. That gave me a bit of comfort, and I was thankful to have friends around, but all I really wanted was Jase. Silent tears flowed down my face and soaked my bedsheet.

As soon as the doctor made the first incision, a nurse named Rhonda said, "Guess who's here?" My view was blocked by a sheet, and I didn't realize she was talking to me, so I didn't respond. Then I heard, "The dad."

I panicked. *Not my dad,* I thought. *I don't want my dad in here. That would be so weird!*

Someone finally said, "Jason," calling my husband by the name most of our friends and family, including me, have always called him.

He walked over to me, peeked behind the sheet, and said, "Hey, babe," then kissed me on the cheek. The minute he entered the operating room, the whole atmosphere changed. It was as though his presence brought a peace and an ease that hadn't been there before.

Jase, in his muddy hunting gear, smelled quite musty and appeared to have blood on his clothes. The doctor wanted him sterile as quickly as possible and was barking orders to him. As an orderly handed him some scrubs, he said to her very calmly, "I washed my hands," as if to say, "Calm down, lady. Everything is okay."

The nurses and I thought his interaction with my doctor was funny. The doctor did not.

The nurses and I also thought the tale of his getting to the hospital was hilarious. He told us that after my first phone call that morning to Miss Kay, she called our neighbor Mac and told him I could be in labor. She wasn't sure yet but wanted to see if Mac could send someone to get Jase just in case it was true. Mac took the situation seriously enough that he immediately sent Chad Johnson, an employee of his cabinet-making business and a good friend of ours, to fetch Jase. Unbeknownst to Miss Kay, Chad took off toward Phil's land in a pirogue, a small canoe-type boat, hoping to locate the blind they were in and get Jase to the hospital. Jase was in the duck blind skinning raccoons, and the next thing he knew, he heard Phil yelling angrily, "Who is this idiot paddling through my decoys?"

Across the water, Chad yelled, "Is Jase in there? His wife is in labor!"

At the news, Jase jumped into the boat, and they paddled back to Phil and Miss Kay's house with the speed of an Olympic rowing team. Jase and Miss Kay hopped in the car and made it to the hospital in seventeen minutes, a trip that usually took about twice that long.

Everyone in the delivery room was laughing at the story, including me. I never knew whether the doctor thought it was funny or not. She certainly did not join in the lightheartedness the rest of us felt. Because my doctor was also one of my bosses, I respected her and yet felt a bit intimidated by her at the same time. Jase was not intimidated at all. He was so relaxed, and that alleviated all the stress and tension I had felt since I first arrived at the hospital. True to his personality, he kept most of the room enthralled and laughing at his stories. As a lifelong hunter, he is no stranger to blood and gore. He thought the surgical process was very interesting and wanted to study everything inside of me. I'm sure his comment that my insides looked like a deer he had skinned the previous day was the first of its kind uttered during a C-section.

At one point, the doctor said to him, "Jason, you have to be quiet now."

"Why?" he asked.

"Because I'm getting close to the baby with this scalpel, and Missy has to stop laughing."

"Oh," he said. "My bad."

As the doctor prepared to remove Cole, the room became quiet; I didn't know exactly what was going on because I couldn't see around the sheet, but I knew the time had come for our baby to be born. Jase watched everything intently. The doctor pulled on the baby, but he would not budge. In Jase's words, "He just wouldn't come out."

So Jase decided to lend a hand. He reached into the area near where the doctor was working, which caused every person to freeze. The room fell completely silent. As Jase recalled later, the doctor's eyes filled with fire, and she shot him laser-sharp looks. No words were spoken, but he immediately raised his hands as if to say, "Don't shoot," and backed off.

The doctor soon realized what was wrong. Cole's umbilical cord was wrapped around his neck—twice. The doctor reached into my uterus and popped it off his neck. As soon as she did, Jase saw Cole flip into her hands, and the doctor was able to deliver him right away.

Despite the trauma of his birth, Cole suffered no residual effects of being tugged on with a cord around his neck while being cut out of the womb. In fact, he let out a loud cry as soon as he took his first breath. He was six pounds, nine ounces, with translucent skin that felt like velvet. He was the most beautiful baby I had ever seen and the softest, warmest bundle I had ever held. His perfectly round head was definitely different from Reed's when he was born. Even though he was only a few minutes old, his cuteness factor was off the charts, and he had a personality to match. We could tell instantly that he would be a sweet, calm, easygoing child. He is still that way to this day.

Cole Foster Robertson has the name Cole because I wanted a one-syllable name, and Jase and I thought Cole was quite original. His middle name, Foster, comes from my well-loved maternal great-grandfather, Bill Foster. Not long after Cole was born, Jase and I realized lots of other parents were naming their sons Cole, perhaps also thinking the name was cool and unusual. It ended up being more common than we had thought, but I cannot imagine him being named anything else.

Once again Jase and I were blessed with a healthy baby boy. Later, as I reflected on the series of events leading up to Cole's grand entrance into the world, I thanked God that His hand had been on everything. From the moment I found out Cole was a breech baby, I didn't hesitate to opt for a C-section rather than have the doctor turn him. Some people might call it a woman's intuition, but I believe it was God guiding me and causing me to feel restless and uneasy about that option. Once Cole was born, I realized that had the doctor turned him with the cord already wrapped twice around his neck, he very well might not have survived.

That's Cole

One of the stories that best illustrates Cole's personality happened when he was three years and two months old. I was still working at the clinic, Reed was attending preschool five days a week, and Jase and I hadn't found anyone to care for Cole while I was gone.

After a season of trial and error, we finally decided Jase would take Cole to work with him a couple of days a week, though the days were rarely consistent. At the time, Duck Commander was still headquartered at Phil and Miss Kay's house, so Miss Kay usually ended up watching Cole while Jase worked, even though she also handled many of the business activities and all of the accounting for the company. I felt so relieved when we finally agreed to that arrangement. I knew Cole was in wonderful hands with his grandmother, and he enjoyed being at his grandparents' house.

I called Jase every day he was supposed to have Cole. Outside of duck hunting season, he left for work after I did, so I never had the satisfaction of seeing him go out the door in the mornings with Cole in tow. I didn't doubt he would take care of Cole, but

I'll admit that I reminded him much more than was necessary: "You have Cole tomorrow. Don't forget, okay?" and "You're taking Cole to work with you today."

On the days Jase had Cole, I couldn't help myself; I called Duck Commander about 11:00 or 11:30 a.m.—just to check in. For some reason, Jase found that annoying. After a couple of weeks of my phone calls, Jase finally said, "Quit checking on me. I know when I'm supposed to have Cole. I got this."

One day, I couldn't resist the urge and called anyway.

"How's Cole?" I asked Jase.

"I don't have Cole," Jase responded.

Wondering if he was teasing me because I had called when I knew I shouldn't have, I said, "You're kidding, right? This is not funny."

"Missy, I'm serious. I really do not have Cole," he said, and I could tell by the tone of his voice that he definitely was not joking. He had left for work without Cole. Our three-year-old was home alone.

Terrified and panicked over where Cole might be or what could have happened to him, I fell out of my office chair and crumpled onto the floor. All sorts of scenarios raced through my mind. Was he hurt? Had he wandered outside when he realized he was home by himself? He could have walked to the road, fallen into a creek, or even been attacked by an animal in the woods. (We lived on about a three-acre lot in a rural area at that time.)

"Today is your day, Jase. You're supposed to have him!" I said, immediately formulating a plan for what to do next.

I called home to see if Cole might answer. Jase called Mac, who worked at home, and asked him to look for Cole. Again, Mac came to our rescue. He jumped into his all-terrain vehicle and raced to our house. A few minutes later, he called Jase back and said, "Cole's fine. I found him standing in your carport, completely dressed, with his jacket on, like he was supposed to go somewhere."

Mac had scooped Cole up in his arms and said, "Hey, Cole. Everything's okay. You're going to come home with me. We're going to call your parents, and your daddy is going to come and get you."

Even though Jase was on his way, I left work, too, determined to make sure Cole was all right.

When I got home and asked him what he did while no one was home, he said, "I looked for you. Then played Nintendo for a while. Then I looked for you some more, but I couldn't find you. I got something to eat and then put my clothes on and went outside."

Once I saw that Cole really was okay and calmed down, I heard Jase's side of the story. He had woken up at the usual time but did not rush to get to work. He made himself breakfast, took out the trash, then got ready for work, all while singing at the top of his lungs, not thinking anyone was around to hear him. He finally left the house around 9:00 a.m. without realizing that Cole was still asleep. Jase didn't think to check on Cole because he thought I had taken him to a babysitter.

Jase says I never told him he was responsible for Cole that day. I have a hard time believing that because Cole's care was at the forefront of my mind every day, and I was very diligent about communicating with whoever would be taking care of him. If anything, my tendency was to overinform people or remind them too many times. Either Jase and I had a major communication problem or one of us had a major memory problem. We still do not know what really happened, but we can laugh about the situation now because everything turned out fine in the end.

I believe Cole is probably the only one of our children who could have handled such circumstances well. He was totally cool with being home alone for almost three hours. His even temper and levelheadedness served him—and us—well that day; and those qualities continue to be a blessing to everyone who knows him. Cole is as mild mannered and laid back as anyone I have ever known. In many ways, he is a lot like Jase. He certainly inherited Jase's analytical nature. Cole is not one to make rash decisions or let his emotions dominate him. He thinks things through, doesn't hurry, and makes the best, most informed decisions he can. He is a loyal friend and family member who is kind and considerate of others, and is definitely a peacemaker.

It's funny how my perspective has changed since I've become a mom—I can't imagine my life without these two young men. I'm grateful that Reed and Cole love each other and are smart and ambitious in their own ways. They both love our family, and more importantly, they both love God and desire to live lives that please and honor Him. They do have several things in common, but their personalities and the ways they choose to do things are completely different. Any parent who has more than one child can definitely relate to this. No two children are alike, and that is what makes life fun and sometimes crazy, but always interesting.

3
"Let's Have Another Baby"

JASE AND I WERE THRILLED with our family that now numbered four. I hadn't completely relinquished my dream of having a daughter someday, but I also needed to fully bounce back from the two complicated births I had gone through.

We settled into a fairly typical routine for a young family. I chose to work part-time so I could be home with the boys as much as possible, allowing me to give them much of my attention and still pick Reed up from school every day and have supper on the table almost every night. The boys spent afternoons playing (and sometimes fighting) with each other. They had to learn how to make their playtime more play than conflict, and I had to learn how to parent two rambunctious, energetic little boys. They spent a good amount of time outside!

Jase went from pitching in fast-pitch softball games every spring to pitching to Reed and Cole in the front yard when he came home from work each night. The dynamics of our family were being set, and all the pieces were falling into place. We didn't have any money left over at the end of the month, nor did we have any type of savings account, but our needs were taken care of, and we were blessed.

Oh No . . .

One afternoon, while I was at home with six-year-old Reed and three-year-old Cole, I could feel a migraine headache starting, a pain I'd felt many times before. After years of suffering with

occasional migraines, I knew how to handle them. If I took medication and a nap as soon as I felt the first twinges of a headache,
I could relieve the symptoms. But that day, there was a problem:
I was out of ibuprofen because I had been having headaches every
day. With two little boys underfoot, I could not take a nap, and
with no medication in the house I knew I was doomed to a severe
migraine episode. I called Jase at Duck Commander and asked
him to bring me some ibuprofen. He said he couldn't leave right
away but would be there as soon as he could.

My headache grew worse. When I realized I was in too much
pain to watch Reed and Cole, I put them in the bathtub with
some toys, where I could see and hear them from my bed. The
idea of being completely unable to care for my sons was extremely frightening to me.

I am not sure Jase understood how serious the headache was
until he arrived home a couple of hours later. When he saw the
boys in the bathtub and realized that I was barely able to move
and had started vomiting, he knew we had a major problem.
The vomiting did relieve some of the tension, and once I took
the ibuprofen I was able to go to sleep. Before I did, I told Jase I
would see the doctor when I got to work the following day.

The migraines had started when I was about eight years old,
soon after I broke my jaw in a bicycle accident and had to have
it wired shut for several weeks. By high school, the migraines had
intensified, and I suffered every month. When I became pregnant
with Reed, they disappeared; the same thing happened when I
was pregnant with Cole. I could not explain the scientific reasons
for this, but I was certain the headaches were somehow related
to hormones.

After the day of the debilitating headache, my doctor suggested

I consider different birth control. I can usually count on Jase to have a creative solution to almost any problem, a notion that does not occur to other people. When I told him the doctor recommended this change, he simply asked, "Why?"

"I can't keep having these headaches every day. I'm not able to function. I have to try something."

Jase offered another idea. "Well, let's have another baby."

Of course! Having another baby would stop the migraines—at least for nine months. At that point, I knew I wanted a third child, but I had not reached the "ready moment" when I believed the time was right and was prepared to act on my desire. But something about the matter-of-fact way Jase suggested it seemed right to me that day. Switching birth control methods was no longer an issue.

What Is Taking So Long?

When Jase and I first decided to start a family, I became pregnant with Reed quickly and easily; the same with Cole. Now I went month after month without conceiving. We were greatly relieved when I finally became pregnant after about eight months.

Several weeks later, on a Saturday evening, Jase and I went to a wedding at church and then to dinner with my parents, who wanted to treat us to a nice meal to celebrate our anniversary. That night, at eight or nine weeks into the pregnancy, I started bleeding and hurting. Not wanting to bother my obstetrician over the weekend, I asked Jase to take me to the emergency room.

In my opinion, the emergency room doctor showed no compassion or gentleness. I can honestly say that after birthing two boys, one without any medication, I experienced the worst pain I had ever felt to date during that examination. Jase was in the room with me and said that watching the doctor examine me was like watching a mechanic work on the engine of a car. "It was brutal," he told me.

At first, all the medical staff told me was, "We think you're having a miscarriage." They did not perform an ultrasound nor give me any pain medicine. They only told me to call my doctor first thing Monday morning and sent me home. I knew I was losing the baby, so I suffered through Sunday as best I could.

On Monday morning my mom went with me to the doctor's office, where they did an ultrasound and determined I had a tubal pregnancy. After almost twelve years of working in the ob-gyn clinic, I had a basic understanding of the term "tubal pregnancy" but did not fully comprehend how it would affect my life that day.

When the doctor said, "I have to go in and remove it," I thought, *Are you serious? You mean you can't transplant the embryo? You can't get it to move down into the uterus? You mean there is nothing you can do to fix it? This is a healthy embryo! Nothing is wrong with this child, and you are telling me you have to remove it?* I could not understand why she offered no options to try to save that baby.

She explained that in a tubal pregnancy the embryo could not travel into the uterus on its own because it had already attached itself to the inside wall of a fallopian tube. "The baby will not survive where it is now, and if we do not take it out, the chances are high that something bad could happen to you."

As my brain began to process what she was saying, I barely heard her next words: "We need to remove it now, and then you need to take the rest of this week off of work."

Before long, I found myself in the preoperative area of the hospital. My mom stayed with me, and soon after Jase, Alan, Lisa, and a family friend arrived.

The thought of having a healthy embryo removed from my body was mind boggling to me. I struggled with it mentally and emotionally until the anesthesia knocked me out completely.

After the procedure, the doctor said, "That was very easily done. I often have to scrape cells and tissue from the tube, but this came out all at once, very cleanly."

I said nothing, but thought, *Maybe it was easy for you. But it's not easy for me. I am an emotional wreck over this whole situation.*

The doctor explained what had caused the tubal pregnancy. As a result of the C-section I had when Cole was born, scar tissue had grown over one of my fallopian tubes and caused it to wrinkle in an accordion-type pattern. Once she snipped the tissue, the tube immediately went back to its normal smooth shape. She then let me know that I should have no problem getting pregnant again and had every reason to expect a normal pregnancy the next time.

It wasn't that easy for my heart. At the time, I felt that surely more could be done to save my baby. But as my doctor had explained, the embryo would not have survived outside the uterus—and leaving it in the fallopian tube could have killed me. Making peace with that reality in my mind, though, might not be possible this side of heaven.

After a week of recuperating at home, I felt fine physically and was ready to return to work. However, the emotional toll of losing a baby still lingered.

∞

Sixteen days later, while working a regular day at the clinic, I felt what seemed like a hunger pang. As the sensation grew more intense, I tried to take the edge off with some peanut butter crackers and a Dr. Pepper, but the snack did not help. In fact, I started feeling worse instead of better. By about noon, I practically had to crawl from my desk into the clinic area to find someone to help me.

"I'm not feeling well. I feel weird," I said to the first nurse I saw.

"Let me get the doctor," she said as she rushed to find my obstetrician.

Within minutes, I was on the ultrasound table with six people looking at the screen, trying to determine what was happening. By that time, I was in tremendous pain, and all I can remember is that there was so much fluid clouding the ultrasound image that no one knew exactly what the problem was.

"Missy," said the doctor, "I'm not sure what is going on here. I have to go in and do another laparoscopy to find out."

Another surgery? I thought. *I just did that—like a couple of weeks ago!*

While my coworkers helped me get into a nurse's van for the short drive to the hospital, someone called Jase to let him know what was happening.

A few minutes after arriving in the same pre-op room I had been in sixteen days earlier, I needed to use the restroom. With the clinic nurse's assistance, I made it there, and when I got inside, I began bleeding profusely.

The Standoff

When I returned from the restroom and Jase saw how much I was bleeding, he began to grill the doctor with every question imaginable. She remained completely stoic, no matter what he said. Every time he asked her a question, she provided the same measured response: "I will not know until I begin to operate."

She began trying to offer various common medical possibilities for this incident, such as a ruptured cyst and other diagnoses. Jase shot down every explanation with the power and speed he would use to blast a duck out of the sky with a shotgun. He was never disrespectful toward her, but he was intense.

Due to the pain I was experiencing, I did not realize exactly what was going on, but I did know I was lying on the bed while the doctor and my husband were in a Western movie standoff on either side of me. These two strong personalities were about to collide, and I was in the direct line of fire! At one point, the telephone in my pre-op room rang. Without saying a word, the doctor picked up the phone, stretched it across my bed, and handed it to Jase, never taking her eyes off his. To say that one could cut the tension in the room with a knife is a complete understatement.

I was not happy about Jase's confrontational manner, but at the same time, I was grateful that he was asking the questions I never thought to ask and telling the doctor exactly how he wanted her to treat me. "Like your own daughter," he said.

Jase clearly communicated that he wanted the doctor to rectify the situation. He went on to tell her, "You better not start taking out a bunch of things that need to be left inside of her. I understand that you have to operate, but *do not remove* anything that does not have to come out." She confirmed her understanding of his expectations and left the room.

"Jason," I said, using his full name, "she is my *boss*." I hated the thought that he might say something to offend her, something that might make my working for her difficult or awkward in the future.

"I don't care," Jase said, "my main concern is you. I am about to send you back into that operating room with her, and I want to make sure she knows my expectations are high."

During the procedure, it was determined that not all of the embryonic tissue had been removed sixteen days earlier and that the remaining cells had reattached to my fallopian tube, started growing again, and eventually ruptured my tube. The doctor removed the damaged part of the tube and left the healthy portion of it. After the operation, I was weak and needed to be cleaned up after bleeding so much earlier that day.

My wonderful sister-in-law Lisa, who has a gift for knowing exactly what people need and when they need it, realized I had to be feeling horrible and physically a mess and said, "Do you want to take a shower?"

"I can't," I replied. "I'm too weak."

Somehow, she managed to get the hospital gown off of me, put me in the shower, and help me wash myself until I was clean. This act of complete selflessness is something I will never forget. No one else thought of this, or if they did, they didn't offer. Lisa knew exactly what I needed and was not timid about jumping in to help me.

I stayed in the hospital that night, exhausted physically and emotionally. Before I left to go home the next day, the doctor told me I needed to stay home to rest for a month. I was shocked. I knew my body and soul had been through a lot, but I did not realize I needed such an extensive recovery.

On the Receiving End

Growing up in the South, especially in a church in the South, I knew what happened when a person was sick, bereaved, recovering from an accident or an operation, or had had a baby: People brought food. Growing up, I had seen this firsthand, and when I became a wife and had a family of my own, I became one of those women in the church who prepared meals for various families. We had been recipients of these meals when I gave birth to each of the boys; people's visits were also excuses for me to get to show off the new baby.

This time was different. There was no baby to show off and absolutely nothing joyful about this recovery. The monthlong time away from my job was supposed to be a *recovery*, meaning lots of rest and little work. I had to face the difficult truth that I could not do everything I wanted to do for my family. With two little boys at home, I was going to have to allow other people to help, whether I liked it or not.

One of the first people to come to my aid during that season was my maternal grandmother. Though she lived out of town, she worked with my mom to hire a lady to come to our home every day, straighten the house, prepare lunch, start dinner, and make sure the boys were taken care of. My grandmother and my mom knew I probably would not have recovered as easily without that kind of help, and they were right. I will always be grateful to my grandmother for her thoughtfulness and generosity when I was still recuperating.

Besides the scheduled meal deliveries our church organized for the first week of my recovery, other friends and family members also brought food and helped us in other practical ways, such as providing transportation for the boys or doing a load of laundry.

Now when I encounter families under stress for some reason, the best advice I can offer to those who want to support them is this: Whatever your gift is, that is what you should do. If you can babysit for a few hours, then babysit. If you can clean house, clean for a family in need. If you can go to the grocery store, go. I encourage people not to shy away from helping others because they do not know what to do or what to say under difficult circumstances. Personally, I never wanted anyone to sit on my sofa and pat my hand, philosophizing about what was happening in our family. We had practical, everyday needs, and I was extremely grateful for anyone who would do anything to help meet those needs and keep our lives going during those days.

This Changes Things

Recovering physically from the second surgery was easier than recovering emotionally. After the first procedure, I bounced back physically fairly quickly and was somewhat encouraged because the doctor indicated I should have no problem becoming pregnant and carrying a healthy baby to term when Jase and I decided to try again. After the second surgery, not only did I still carry the sadness and disappointment of losing a baby, I now had to wrestle with the fact that a portion of one of my fallopian tubes had been removed, and the chances of conceiving again were slim. It was not impossible, but it was not likely.

I swung back and forth between grieving for the unknown child Jase and I had been hoping for and trying to force myself to be happy with the two healthy sons we already had. After a while, I finally realized that mourning the loss of having any more children overshadowed the blessings that were already in my life. I chose to focus on what I did have—not on what I did not have—and that decision strengthened me and grounded me in the wake of the potential loss of our dream of another baby.

"I'm What?"

At the end of September, I was ready to go back to work at the clinic. I had decided not to resume any type of birth control. I knew that getting pregnant again was not likely with only one functional fallopian tube; and I remembered how long it had taken for me to conceive when I stopped taking the pills about a year earlier. *The chances that I'll get pregnant again are not very high*, I'd thought repeatedly, *but if it ever does happen, that will be great.*

As much as I enjoyed being back in the office, juggling places for Cole to stay while I was at work and the stress I had endured emotionally and physically during the previous months began to take their toll. The time was right to make a change.

For a few years, Miss Kay had been asking me to come work for Duck Commander. I loved my job at the clinic, so I put her off year after year. But now it made perfect sense.

In late December 2002, I resigned from the clinic after twelve fulfilling years, grateful for the doctors and colleagues who had not only made my time pleasant while I worked there but had also treated me like family through two difficult birth experiences, a lost pregnancy, and two surgeries. A few weeks later, I found myself in a work atmosphere completely different from the structured environment at the clinic—a small, laid-back family business that produced and distributed duck calls.

The first responsibility of my new job was to prepare the paperwork and duck call samples for our annual meeting with the Wal-Mart buyer at the company's headquarters in Bentonville, Arkansas. Jase was driving in from Texas, where he had been hunting and filming with Phil. The Wal-Mart presentation was the most important meeting for our company each year, as their order alone would ensure that we could all be paid for the next twelve months.

Since Jase and I hadn't seen each other for nearly a week and knowing he would not be able to come home for a few more days, he and I had one wonderfully romantic night staying at the Holiday Inn and eating cheese fries, all on the company credit card. Pure luxury for young parents on a tight budget!

A few weeks later, I was completely unprepared for the familiar sensations I began to feel. Having been pregnant three times before, I knew the symptoms, and I definitely had them. Jase and I were surprised and overjoyed when the pregnancy test showed "positive," but we thought we would be wise to proceed with caution, so we kept the happy news to ourselves as long as possible.

Yet Another Challenge

Several weeks into the pregnancy, I received an unsettling telephone call from my doctor. "We have a problem," she told me. She went on to explain a medical condition I knew nothing about, a condition that could pose a serious threat for my unborn child.

This medical problem, called Rh incompatibility, is complicated, but I will try to make it easy to understand. My blood type is A-negative, so I am an Rh-negative patient. This is important for every woman to know, because if you have negative blood, you need to receive a Rhogam shot at twenty-eight weeks' gestation of every pregnancy and receive another Rhogam shot after every birth, miscarriage, or tubal pregnancy in order to avoid the potential for horribly adverse problems with future pregnancies.

During this phone call, the doctor informed me that I had not received a Rhogam shot after the tubal pregnancy; therefore, our new baby was at risk if he or she had positive blood. The antibodies in Rhogam neutralize the mother's blood type with the baby's, and without it, my body would treat the baby as a foreign object and attempt to eliminate it. This would result in a probable miscarriage, unless the baby's blood type was also negative.

I wondered if I could take the shot after I had already conceived, but I learned it would have no effect, and I now found myself in an extremely high-risk pregnancy. I tried to absorb everything the doctor was telling me and finally said to her, "Okay, I hear what you are trying to tell me. I needed the shot before I got pregnant. But since I did not get it, what is going to happen? What do we do?"

"Our goal is to get this baby to twenty-six weeks," she said.

My jaw dropped. "What happens at twenty-six weeks?" I asked, still reeling from the news of this completely unexpected and frightening development.

"At that point, we'll do a C-section because the baby will have a better chance of surviving outside your body than in the womb."

The only scenario to ensure that the pregnancy would progress without difficulty was for the baby's blood type to be negative. Jase's blood type is O-positive (with a recessive Rh-negative factor), which is why Reed and Cole were both positive, as was the baby lost in the tubal pregnancy. We had no reason to expect anything different with this baby.

"Is there any possibility at all that this baby will have negative blood?" I asked the doctor, hoping against hope.

"It's not impossible since Jase is also carrying a negative factor. But I've never seen it happen."

Before the end of the phone call, my doctor told me she had

never treated a patient with this condition but would follow my situation carefully. "I'll do some research on this," she said, "and I will call you back. We will take good care of you and do our very best to make this a viable pregnancy."

I responded with resolve. "Tell me what to do, and I will do it."

She did not say much more, except to let me know that she would look into my condition and get back to me.

I was devastated.

This Was Not My Fault

I hoped my doctor's promised research would result in a report of some new discovery or little-known solution to our problem—anything to help us. As day after day passed while we waited to hear from her, I grew increasingly concerned. My nature is to face every challenge with a plan to overcome it, and the longer I waited for information, the less time I had to formulate a strategy.

A full week after the doctor's initial phone call, I still had not heard anything from her. Frustrated to still be waiting on instructions that could impact my baby's well-being, I left a message at the clinic, asking her to return my call. When she called later that day, her words were crisp and short, and her tone seemed flippant as she told me she had not had time to research my situation. I was shocked at this change in her attitude—a far cry from being kind or considerate.

Totally stunned that she had done absolutely nothing to investigate a course of action *and* that she seemed annoyed at my very asking, I said good-bye to her, hung up the telephone, redialed the clinic number, and asked for the head nurse.

I explained to her what had transpired during the two phone

calls and asked (well, more like demanded) to switch doctors. My request was immediately approved.

When I told Jase about the phone call, he was as upset as I was. We knew none of this was my fault. I had needed a Rhogam shot after the tubal pregnancy—both times—and had not received it. With all the drama and the complications of that situation, I could understand how someone might forget once. But twice? She was the doctor; wasn't it her job to remember what to do?

Attorneys convinced Jase and me that we had a legal case, but I was very reluctant to proceed with this process. The clinic had been like home to me for twelve years, and I could not imagine cutting off my ties with everyone there. I persuaded Jase to wait for the outcome of this pregnancy before we decided on our next step. He reluctantly agreed.

What Are the Chances?

I immediately felt at ease during the first appointment with my new ob-gyn, Dr. Davis. I was confident she would do everything in her power to help me deliver a healthy baby. I asked her the same question I had asked my former doctor: "Is there even the slightest chance this baby will have negative blood?"

Dr. Davis basically reiterated the same answer I had already received. "There is a very small possibility, but it's not likely, Missy." That was all I needed to hear. Immediately, my heart grabbed on to a hope I had not known before. That was something Jase and I could pray for, and we started praying intensely right away.

One of the first steps Dr. Davis took was to send me to a specialist from Louisiana State University who periodically saw patients in Monroe. I saw him at a local hospital every three weeks. Each visit, he ordered an ultrasound and drew blood for a special type of lab work that would monitor the antibodies in my blood. The markers in the blood work would indicate how severely the Rh incompatibility was affecting our unborn child. The doctors had told us that the number would rise as the pregnancy progressed and that when it reached a certain critical point, hopefully not before twenty-six weeks, the obstetrician would need to take the baby by C-section. We hoped and prayed fervently that would not happen.

4

Victory against the Odds

MY VISITS TO THE SPECIALIST should have produced high anxiety, and in the beginning they did. But as the weeks passed, Jase and I, along with our family and friends, continued to pray that even though the odds were stacked against our baby, he or she would not be adversely affected by the Rh incompatibility. We were greatly encouraged when the numbers in the blood work had not risen as the doctors expected, and I thought, *Wow, our prayers are really working. These levels are staying down.*

When I asked Dr. Davis what she thought about the low levels, she said, "There's no explanation for this, Missy, except one: The baby must have negative blood."

I could hardly speak.

I admit that though our family and others were praying for this unlikely outcome, I did not really expect it to happen. An important lesson I had heard all of my life became deeply personal that day: God hears and answers prayer. He does not need good odds. He can make the impossible possible and bring a victory when the chances seem insurmountable.

After a few weeks, all of my doctors concluded our baby must definitely have a negative blood type. That was the only medical reason for the stability of the blood levels. Dr. Davis discontinued my visits to the specialist and began treating me as she would treat any other expectant mother. She was attentive to the potential complication, but it was no longer a major issue. Jase and I were so relieved!

At twenty weeks, with the uncertainty and trauma of the past five months finally behind us, we were so excited about the ultrasound that would reveal our baby's gender. When we found out we were having a baby girl, we were elated. I finally felt free to reconnect with the dreams I once had of being able to dress my daughter in beautiful clothes, give her dolls, and decorate a sweet, feminine bedroom for her. I could hardly wait.

Another Look

For the next several weeks, we relaxed and began the exciting task of coming up with possible names for our daughter. With the boys old enough to contribute their own suggestions, we had all kinds of names being thrown at us, some good, some not-so-good. One day, Cole told me he liked the name Mia.

"Where did you hear that name, Cole?" I asked my five-year-old.

"I don't remember," he said, "but I think it's pretty."

I personally was leaning toward the name Sophie. Jase liked both suggestions but couldn't make a final decision on either one. Jase had excused himself from introducing potential baby names because of the ridicule he had received after trying to name Reed "Cypress Creek."

A few days later, I took Reed and Cole to McDonald's before going to a movie. While we were at McDonald's, I heard a mom trying to get a child's attention in the playground, calling her Sophie. *Aw, that's the name I like.* A little while later at the movie theater, a child hollered to another child, "Sophie, wait up!" That was the decision-making factor for me. The name Sophie was out of the question. I wanted a name that was different from most children (like I thought I was getting with Cole), and the day's events were a clear sign for me.

When I got home that day, I announced to Jase and the boys that our baby girl was going to be named Mia. Later, when I mentioned the name to Lisa, she thought it was appropriate— Mia would now be an acronym for "Made in Arkansas!" We also decided to keep the tradition of the middle name being from a family member and chose my mom's middle name, Elaine.

With the burden of the Rh complications lifted, we began to prepare for Mia's arrival with light hearts and great enthusiasm. We even took a trip to the beach and had a wonderful time. Even now I flip through the photographs from that vacation and realize how much I still treasure the looks of happiness on all our faces.

The week after we returned from our beach getaway, at thirty-one weeks' gestation, I was scheduled for another ultrasound, one using a remarkable new four-dimensional (4-D) technology that would give us an amazingly detailed look at Mia. I was excited about getting to see our daughter's tiny features up close. After so many anxious ultrasounds during my visits to the specialist, being able to have one without any concern was a welcome relief.

Since Jase had been with me for the twenty-week scan when we found out we were having a girl, he decided to forgo it this time and let others join in the excitement. I thought this ultrasound would be an easy, fun opportunity to give the boys a glimpse of their new sister, and while Jase would be missed, he could watch the video that night at home. Miss Kay, Lisa, and Jessica all wanted to see our baby girl, too, so they went with the boys and me to the clinic that day.

The ultrasound room was abuzz with happy anticipation as the technician, a former coworker of mine, prepared for the scan. Miss Kay described it as "a completely joyous time." As the image of Mia's face became clear on the screen, we were ooh-ing and aah-ing and commenting on how cute her little cheeks were. Then the adults in the room grew quiet. The technician ran the ultrasound wand over the same spot several times, trying unsuccessfully to conceal her growing concern.

"Does her nose look smushed to you?" I asked, already knowing in my heart that it did not look normal and that something was wrong.

She simply said, "I need to get the doctor."

My eyes filled with tears.

The instant Miss Kay perceived there was a problem, she sprang into action, and she and Jessica herded the boys out of the room. I do not remember what she said to them, perhaps something she knew they would not resist, such as "Let's go get something to eat!" I knew they were in good hands.

Over the next several minutes, the technician returned with Dr. Davis and was busy trying to capture as many photos and as much video of the baby's facial features as possible. Lisa called Jase, who immediately began heading to the hospital. Dr. Davis viewed the ultrasound and confirmed my worst fears—something, indeed, was wrong. She referred to the baby's condition as a cleft lip. Even with advanced technology, the scan could not reveal whether or not the palate was also cleft.

Dr. Davis wanted to meet with Jase and me as soon as he arrived at the clinic. Lisa stayed with me in a waiting room where Jase was going to meet us. I was so uncomfortable. A public waiting room was the last place I wanted to be after receiving bad news, but I tried to be as strong as possible.

When Jase found us and we began to talk about this new development, he tried to encourage me by saying, "We'll just have to teach her that beauty is on the inside."

I was furious over that comment, but I did not respond because I was trying my best to keep from breaking down. His intentions were good, but his timing stunk! I had just received the news about our baby's cleft lip thirty minutes earlier and was still in denial, hoping the situation would somehow change. I had not yet accepted it, and Jase's words indicated to me that he had bought into it completely. The first thing I wanted to do was pray that the baby would be healed in the womb, and I felt Jase's comment completely ignored that possibility.

His words made me livid that day, but since then, they have been a source of strength and a lifeline for me in many different situations we have been through with Mia. I hated them when he said them; I cherish them now.

What Exactly Are We Dealing With?

During the twelve years I had worked at the ob-gyn clinic, I had only heard of one other cleft-lip situation and knew almost nothing about a cleft palate. Over the following weeks, I would learn more than I ever dreamed I could know, much of it very daunting.

When I scanned the Mayo Clinic's website, I found a very simple definition of cleft lip and palate: "Cleft lip and cleft palate are openings or splits in the upper lip, the roof of the mouth (palate) or both. Cleft lip and cleft palate result when the facial structures that are developing in an unborn baby don't close completely."[2] As I looked at other websites such as WebMD, I began to comprehend the significant differences between cleft lip and cleft palate.[3] The more I read, the more I realized that a cleft lip is a medical situation that must be addressed, but a cleft palate is a far more serious condition.

I have always been the type of person who deals best with difficulty by getting busy. When something highly emotional or intensely demanding hits my life, I take a basic approach: Give me a week to get my mind around this, then get out of my way.

The first obstacle we had to clear was to inform our family and friends of the baby's condition. That was extremely difficult for me. To know the truth in my heart and mind was one thing. To voice it aloud to those around me was heart wrenching. Thankfully, Miss Kay is good about spreading news, especially a situation that needs prayer. She not only prays but she is an expert at enlisting other people to pray too. Knowing she would make sure the right people found out what they needed to know took tremendous pressure off of me.

By the end of the first week after the 4-D ultrasound, I had begun to process what Jase and I were dealing with. I had done as much grieving as I could do at that point, and I was ready to get to work. As a task-oriented person, gathering information, looking for options, and identifying possible solutions for Mia would help me more than anything else. So those were the things I wanted to do.

In addition to researching cleft lip and palate, I found a tremendous resource in Jase's cousin Melissa. She is his first cousin on his father's side, and I had gotten to know her well when she lived with us for two years while finishing college. She helped us tremendously during the time I was pregnant with Cole and after he was born. As soon as Melissa heard about our baby's diagnosis, she called me and said, "Here's what we need to do."

Several years earlier, Melissa had earned her degree in speech therapy. I had no idea how valuable her training would be until she began to explain the speech challenges faced by children with cleft lip and palate. Until then, I had focused almost exclusively on the physical aspects of the condition.

Knowing we would need extensive medical services, Melissa contacted a large medical center in south Louisiana, not too far from our home. When the staff member never returned her call, Melissa secured an appointment for us at another medical center in Arkansas, this one specializing in the care of children. We met with an ear, nose, and throat doctor for almost an hour. She was very informative, and I grew more and more comfortable with her as the conversation progressed. She was definitely well versed in the field of cleft lips and palates, and I had almost decided that this is where we were going to bring our baby.

Then I asked, "Will you be doing the surgeries?"

"I'll be in the room," she said.

I was confused. "Then who will be operating?"

"Well, this *is* a teaching hospital. Students will be doing the operation."

I looked at Melissa, whose jaw was open and whose eyes were like saucers, and said, "Not on my baby."

We quickly stood up, thanked the doctor for her time, and left. By this time, I was thirty-four weeks along, and Dr. Davis had told me I could no longer travel. Completely discouraged and becoming more and more stressed without a plan to help my daughter, I felt helpless.

∞

The following Sunday morning Jase's brother Alan, who was a minister at our church at that time, began his sermon by informing the congregation about our situation. He gave them enough basic information so they would have an understanding of what we were facing and asked everyone to be in prayer for our baby and our family. We knew he had planned to address the church on our behalf, but we were not prepared for how difficult it would be for us, sitting there and listening to someone else talk about what we were going through. We felt that all the eyes in the room were on us. Of course, their eyes were filled with kindness and support, being our family and friends, but we simply were not accustomed to having our lives on display. The focus on us felt warm and loving, yet totally new and a bit uncomfortable at the same time.

We were grateful for the prayers and well wishes from our church family, but we were also aware that we had a long and perhaps grueling journey ahead of us. Before we left the building that Sunday, a woman we had known for years approached us and said, "I have a client whose grandson was born with this condition a few months ago. May I give her your phone number?"

"Yes! Please do!" we replied, happy and relieved by the possibility of connecting with another family who had already walked the path we were set to travel. Better yet, the family did not live far from us. We had been discouraged that week because of the dead ends we encountered at two major hospitals, so we were desperate to speak to someone—*anyone*—who had experience with cleft situations.

A Godsend

Our friend at church did contact the family she knew, and the mother of the baby, Amy Stegall, called me that night. The tone in her voice was not at all what I expected. She was not sad, discouraged, or frustrated. Her voice had a ring of joy to it, and everything she said to me was encouraging. I could tell immediately that Amy was a go-getter and a problem solver, a kindred spirit for me. I listened, more hopeful than ever, as she said, "We have found the best place on earth for our baby. I would love for you to meet our son, and then I can tell you more about his doctors."

We made plans for Amy and her six-month-old son, Bolton, to visit me at home later that week. As I hung up the phone, I felt better about our situation than I had ever felt. I hoped and believed Amy had the answers and resources our family needed.

Several days later, Amy and precious little Bolton showed up on our doorstep. I was thrilled to see them. Bolton had been through one surgery at that point and was preparing for another procedure fairly soon. Amy gave me mounds of information that day, the most important piece of which was the name of the International Craniofacial Institute (ICI) in Dallas, Texas, and the renowned surgeon based there, Dr. Kenneth Salyer. At that time, Dr. Salyer had recently gained global attention when he surgically separated a set of conjoined twins from Egypt.

Amy also shared with me the detailed process she and her husband undertook to identify ICI as the best place for Bolton's care and Dr. Salyer as the best surgeon for him. Amy's husband had researched many physicians and surgeons on the Internet and finally narrowed their choices to two by asking one important question: Which doctors have been published on the subject of cleft lip and palate?

Ultimately, they chose Dr. Salyer. Once I heard about how thorough their research was and how happy they were with the entire team at ICI, I knew I needed to contact the Institute. I had only one question for Amy: "Will they take us? It sounds like this Dr. Salyer is kind of big time."

She could not answer that, of course, but she did give me his e-mail address and encouraged me to write to him directly. *But he's famous*, I thought. *Will he even look at an e-mail from me?*

I couldn't let my moment of self-doubt keep me from seeking the best possible care for our baby, so I quickly sent a message to Dr. Salyer. I explained to him that an ultrasound of our baby had revealed a cleft lip, but we did not know whether or not the palate was involved. At the time, everything was so new to me that I spelled *palate* the same way we spelled it for the wooden platforms we used at Duck Commander—*pallet*. After briefly explaining our baby's condition to the doctor, I asked, "What will it take for you to be willing to take our baby as a patient?"

I was thrilled when he replied to my message the next day with the instruction to contact his new patient coordinator, Sue, giving me the phone number where I could reach her. I called her right away.

"What do we do?" I asked.

"Just call us as soon as the baby is born," she said. "We will make an appointment to see you when she is about a week old. You don't need to do anything else before the baby comes."

What did she say? Do nothing? This was extremely difficult for me; I had an innate need to work on fixing our dilemma, but I had no choice. I followed Sue's orders. In the meantime, I asked Melissa to do some research on Dr. Salyer since she was determined we should seek a physician who considered a child's speech development just as important—or even more so—as that child's outward appearance. She was pleased with what she found.

A visit to the Institute before Mia came was not possible. I was a bit nervous about moving forward with them without seeing the facility or meeting any of the staff. Sue had also told me during the phone call that the Institute would not take our insurance, meaning that instead of 80 percent–20 percent coverage, we could expect only 60 percent–40 percent coverage. Despite that major setback, I believed in my heart that God had led us there through the Stegalls, so in faith, I told Sue that we would call her as soon as possible after the delivery.

More Important than Money

Knowing the International Craniofacial Institute did not take the type of insurance Jase and I had was a source of anxiety for us, to say the least. As a budget-oriented couple who never believed in living beyond our means, this additional layer of stress made our situation even more difficult than it already was for us. We had no credit card debt because we were the kind of people who never bought anything if we did not have the money for it. We did owe money on our house and our cars, but we made our payments in full and on time every month. Just the thought of the travel expenses alone of going back and forth to Dallas concerned me.

But we could not allow our lack of financial resources to determine our course of action. We could not wait and hope the situation would get better on its own somehow; we *had* to seek medical care. We prayed about what to do for our daughter, and once we realized ICI was the best option for her, we knew it was our *only* option. So we decided we would do the very best we could for Mia and trust God with the costs of her care. This was a tremendous step of faith for us because we were determined to pay the Institute whatever we owed them, no matter how much, and no matter how long it took.

We did not go into the situation hoping the Institute would write off any of our bill or trying to figure out how we could get a discount. From my experience working in a doctor's office, I knew we could end up with a huge bill, but I also knew we could make payment arrangements with them and would do our best to pay it on time month after month. I knew the chances were high that Jase and I would still be sending one hundred dollars a month to Dallas when we were old and gray. If that happened, we would make our payments faithfully and be okay with doing so.

It wasn't an easy decision for Jase. He immediately thought, *It really doesn't matter how many zeros are behind the numbers on the bills. It will be a black hole for us no matter how much it is. It won't take many doctor visits or surgeries to wipe us out.* But then he focused on Mia, who needed our help. He concluded, "We will probably be in debt for the rest of our lives, but we are going to get our daughter the best care we can find. All that matters is making sure our little girl has the best possible chance for a happy, healthy life."

Finding the words to tell Reed and Cole what to expect when their little sister was born was another harrowing task. *What exactly will an eight-year-old and a five-year-old understand about this situation?* I wondered. *Will they be scared? How much will this affect their lives?* All these questions swirled in my mind on a daily basis, and I dreaded this conversation with them.

Finally, I sat both of them down and told them that their sister was going to be born different from other babies, that she would look different because her face did not grow together in my tummy like theirs did. I took them to the computer and showed them before-and-after photos of some of Dr. Salyer's patients, which were on his website. They looked at each one with curious eyes but didn't react the way I expected. There were even a few "awws" and an "Oh, he's so cute." Wow, what hope and encouragement those two little boys gave me that day! They saw right past the imperfection and into the spirit of each of those babies. After we looked at the pictures, they ran right back into their playroom and continued playing.

One More Day

Mia was due near the end of September 2003. When I went to Dr. Davis for a regular obstetrics check on September 11, my blood pressure was extremely high and I was unusually swollen.

"You're down to the last three weeks," Dr. Davis said, "and your blood pressure is too high. We need to take this baby."

I panicked. I told Dr. Davis that my dad was preaching for a week out of state, far enough away that it would take hours for my parents to get back to West Monroe, possibly not until the following day. With my dad scheduled to preach every night, I knew he would not be able to leave, but I also knew my mom would do everything in her power to get to me. With everything we had already been through with this baby and everything we anticipated facing in the weeks and years to come, I really wanted her to be there for the birth. In addition, I did not want to have the baby on 9/11, as the terrorist attacks on the United States had happened only two years earlier, and the heart of our nation was still raw and broken over that date.

"Okay," said Dr. Davis. "Call your mom and tell her to get here as quickly as possible. Then go home and get in bed. Do not get up except to go to the bathroom. If you feel bad or strange in any way, call me immediately."

I was very grateful that Dr. Davis was willing to wait a day to deliver the baby. She scheduled the C-section for September 12 at 11:30 a.m. That was all I needed for now—one day for my mom to get home and for the date on the calendar to change.

5
Our Baby Girl!

THERE'S SOMETHING ABOUT PREPARING a room for a new baby girl that is especially exciting for most mothers, and I was no exception. Something about the softness, the daintiness, and the frills and femininity of decorating for a daughter was very special to me. When we first found out we were having a girl, I was especially looking forward to two things—dressing her in beautiful clothes and designing a beautiful nursery for her.

Once we found out about Mia's cleft, though, I had to spend a lot of time learning about the medical aspects we would face once she was born, and while I continued to shop for her, I could not devote as much time as I had hoped to designing a sweet, comfortable room. Besides, finances were tight for Jase and me, and we knew we would soon be facing many more medical bills than usual with a newborn.

Thankfully, Miss Kay loves to shop and decorate, and she was eager to help with her new granddaughter's room. She and Phil did not have much money then either, but she was happy to sacrifice other things to help me with Mia.

One day Miss Kay had scheduled me to work at Duck Commander until late in the afternoon. When I arrived home, I could hardly believe my eyes. Without my knowing it, she had arranged a complete makeover of Mia's room. My sister-in-law Korie, Melissa, and some of my friends had completely transformed it. The walls were painted a beautiful mint green, several pieces of furniture I already owned had been painted white, my great-great-grandmother's rocking chair had been reupholstered, and the new white baby bed Miss Kay had bought for us was covered with pink and white linens. In addition, Miss Kay had found an antique baby carriage and filled it with knickknacks and books to accessorize the room.

Walking into that room for the first time was extremely emotional for me. My family and friends had spent an entire day working hard to surprise me and bless Mia, and Miss Kay—knowing she could do nothing to change the medical challenges we were facing, did what she does best—provided comfort in tangible ways. I was so proud of that room that day and for years afterward. Every time I entered it, I sensed the love of the people close to us. For eight years, except for getting another bed when Mia outgrew the original one, I left the room close to the way it was the day I first saw it, keeping the same love-crafted decor even when we moved everything to a new house during that time.

When I asked Miss Kay recently about her choice of decor, she said, "I was drawn to antiques for Mia's room. For some reason, when I thought about her, I also thought about the pioneers. I could not get away from remembering everything I had heard about the pioneer spirit, the attitudes that enabled people to go through hard times and pull together and fight and overcome their obstacles. When I went antiquing and saw pretty, old things for Mia's room, all I could think was, *She's going to have a pioneer spirit. Certain things are not going to be easy for her, but she is going to pull through it all and overcome her challenges and be a blessing to a lot of people.*

Miss Kay was exactly right about her granddaughter. Almost

immediately after Mia was born, Miss Kay and the rest of our family would recognize her strength.

September 12, 2003

Although I had already given birth to two babies, including a C-section with Cole, something about our daughter's birth felt surreal to me. I remember being wheeled into the operating room, but then everything seemed to happen in slow motion. Maybe one reason it seemed unusual was that Cole's birth had happened so quickly and with a lot of stress, only to be relieved by laughter and excitement when Jase barely made it to the hospital from the duck blind. Mia's birth was filled with anxiety and questions—specifically, whether God had healed her in the womb as we had been praying for, and if not, how severe her cleft was.

Dr. Davis and Jase were the first two people to see Mia once she was delivered. I knew we were dealing with the worst-case scenario when I heard Dr. Davis's tone of voice as she said, "Oh, Missy, she's beautiful." To me, her comment sounded more consoling than joyous and relieved. I instantly thought, *She doesn't know what else to say. She's probably trying to prepare me for the considerable facial defects that our baby has.*

I had not seen my baby girl yet because I was behind a sheet. Eager to hear Jase say something, anything, I called his name: "Jase . . ."

"It's the lip *and* the palate," he said, knowing I needed to hear the truth. He was right.

Within the first minute or so of Mia's life, I heard her cry. She did not take an extremely long time to utter her first sound, but long enough for me to think her cry was a bit delayed. When she did make a noise, it was not the strong cry many babies make.

Even though her cry was less robust than that of other newborns, someone in the room said it was still healthy.

Dr. Davis held her up for me to catch my first glimpse of our six-pound, nine-ounce baby girl. At that moment, she opened her mouth wide and I could see the crater where the roof of her mouth should have been. I knew in that instant that our entire family had begun a long journey that would be quite difficult and painful at times.

Within seconds after Mia had cried, I realized that things seemed to be turning chaotic in the room. "What's going on?" I asked. No one answered. I heard snatches of conversation among the medical staff who were rushing Mia out of the room. All I could understand was something about her not breathing. I could tell that Jase was torn between staying with me and going with Mia.

"I'm fine," I told him. "Go with Mia!"

Lying on that gurney while Dr. Davis finished sewing me up and not having any idea what was happening with my baby was excruciating. I silently prayed for God to intervene in Mia's life at that very moment. While the pediatrician and medical staff were working on Mia, Jase was asked to wait outside.

In the waiting room, our family and friends were anxiously watching for Jase to appear, just as he had twice before with our boys. This time there was no baby in his arms. He opened the door and saw thirty-five to forty people, all waiting with questions in their eyes. Not knowing Mia's condition and seeing the size of the crowd left him speechless and teary eyed.

Jim Moran, one of the elders from our church, led a prayer with the whole group. This is what our church family does. They show up. They pray. They serve. To this day, I don't know who all was in that waiting room, and I'm not sure Jase can even remember, but I do know that none of them were there for themselves. They were there to support us, to let us know that they loved us and were there if we needed them. Jase needed them at that very moment.

Because of the various conditions and complications that can be associated with cleft lip and palate, Mia could have had a serious condition, though Jase and I did not know that at the time. We had no idea what was going on with our baby behind those closed doors. Was something wrong with her lungs? Had they not developed just as her mouth had not developed? Was she unable to process oxygen for some reason and subsequently not able to breathe at all? The previous thoughts of dealing with the ramifications of having a child born with a cleft were quickly set aside. Jase and I were now consumed with praying—no, begging—God to deliver our baby girl to us.

Thankfully, the medical staff soon discovered her breathing troubles were due to "wet lungs," a somewhat usual occurrence after a C-section, in which a newborn consumes amniotic fluid during the procedure. Normally, an infant would not be rushed to the neonatal intensive care unit (NICU) for wet lungs, but the doctor sent Mia there out of an abundance of caution.

Even though Mia's issue with her lungs was relatively common, medically speaking, it was not common to Jase and me. A few minutes later, a relieved Jase reentered the surgical area with the update that the medical team had diagnosed her with wet lungs. We were overwhelmingly grateful.

My mom arrived at the hospital while I was in recovery. She entered while the on-call neonatologists were educating me on my new baby's condition. However, I quickly realized that these specialists were nowhere near up-to-date on their knowledge of cleft lip and palate. One of the doctors told me that my baby's cleft lip would be repaired in about a year and the palate would be repaired at about the eighteen-month mark. When I told her that actually the lip would be repaired at three months and the palate between six and eight months (something I learned from talking to Sue at ICI and from reading on the Institute's website), the doctor replied in what I considered a very patronizing tone. "No, one year for the lip and eighteen months for the palate." Instead of arguing with someone who was unaware of the advances that had been made in recent years regarding this condition, I passively said, "Okay, thank you."

These "specialists" left the room, and Jase and I shrugged. That experience only reinforced our decision to drive Mia the four and a half hours to ICI, the place we knew was right for her.

Love at First Sight

Once a baby enters the NICU, getting him or her out is not easy. After I spent time in the recovery room and then was moved to a regular room, I asked a nurse, "Would you bring my baby to me, please?"

"I'm sorry," she replied. "Your daughter has to stay in the NICU until she meets certain physical standards." NICU is not like a normal baby nursery, where babies can be taken in and out and friends and family can see her through a window. Only immediate family members—two at a time—are permitted in the NICU. That meant all of our extended family and friends who came to support us and see Mia when she was born went home without even getting a glimpse of her. But the staff reassured us that once Mia was well enough to leave the NICU, she was well enough to go home.

Jase and I quickly learned that the standards Mia had to meet before she was released would be quite challenging for her. She would need to consume a certain number of ounces of formula each day, but we did not know whether she would be able to suck since she did not have the roof of her mouth.

To make matters worse, because I had undergone a C-section I was subject to the hospital's postoperative rules. One of those rules was that I could not leave my room until the next day. Since Mia could not leave the NICU and I could not leave my room, both of us lost important, precious bonding moments together during the first hours of her life. Every time I thought about her lying in an incubator all alone with no one to comfort her, it tore me up inside. Fortunately, Jase didn't miss a minute of visiting hours that first day. He and my mom grabbed every opportunity they could to see Mia during the first twenty-four hours of her life.

My mom took pictures of Mia in the NICU and brought them to me in my room—a sad substitute for actually being able to hold and talk to my baby but the best anyone could do. In one of the photos, Mom had put a stuffed animal into Mia's bed with her. Because I knew how small the plush toy was, I could easily figure out how tiny Mia was.

The next day a nurse offered to roll me to the NICU to see Mia for the first time. The anticipation of that visit made my heart churn with so much love and so many questions. I did not like the idea of having to be pushed in a wheelchair (again, hospital rules) or the thought of being seen by other people in the hospital. As the nurse rolled me past other parents with healthy babies, I could feel their sympathy, as though each one was thinking, *Oh, that poor lady. She doesn't have her baby.*

Though the lights in the NICU were dim, I saw Mia clearly, hooked up to various tubes and wires. But I also noticed that she was not connected to nearly as many tubes as other infants were. This gave me an immediate sense of comfort and gratitude.

When I leaned next to her, I was surprised that her mouth was closed. She was sleeping like any other baby, peaceful and content. The cleft in her lip looked like little more than two minor cuts, which made me wonder for a brief moment if she might really be okay. But the appearance of the cuts betrayed the serious problems inside her mouth, problems I knew would take surgeries to correct. Still, having tried to prepare myself emotionally for the severity of how her mouth might look, in that moment, I was shocked to hear myself say in the privacy of my heart, "She *is* beautiful."

Tough Timing

Because Mia was born earlier than expected, she was in the NICU during teal season. A type of duck, teals migrate about two months earlier than other ducks, so the two hunting seasons are separate. From my perspective, teal season is as demanding as duck season. Jase's hours at home are just as short, and the stress he feels is just as high. As I explained previously, hunting was a major source of food and income for our family at that time in our lives, and Jase could not simply skip teal season because we had a baby in the hospital—any more than a doctor could stop seeing patients or a firefighter could decide not to fight fires. Jase's missing work was not an option for us. Besides, the duck blind was where his dad, uncle, and other good friends were every morning. I knew that these men were a huge source of comfort and encouragement to Jase during this time, and he needed that. We both did.

Every night, Jase came to the hospital and slept on an uncomfortable vinyl pullout bed until about 4:00 a.m., when he'd leave to go hunting. I was traumatized and extremely emotional over Mia's situation, and although being at the hospital at night was stressful for Jase, he wanted to be there. He was so torn between the need to make a living and the desire to be with his family.

My parents kept Reed and Cole that week, and the most difficult part of being separated from them was that Reed had a school project due that I had planned to work on with him. He was looking forward to molding a dinosaur from clay, and I was looking forward to it too. Having my mom step in and help Reed was difficult for me to accept—not because she wasn't capable, but because I wanted so much to keep being a good mother to Reed and Cole, even though I was facing the biggest challenge of my life.

My parents took excellent care of the boys, and in the end, the dinosaur project turned out wonderfully. Reed had been envisioning everything in his head for some time; he knew *exactly* how he wanted it to look and was determined to recreate his vision. The only help he needed was finding the right creative materials at the store. I think the project helped take his mind off of my being at the hospital and temporarily put aside his own worries about his new little sister.

When Can We Leave?

The NICU was equipped with all kinds of specialized bottles for infants with clefts. They had bottles with accessories to pump milk directly into the mouth and bottles with custom nipples designed for cleft conditions. Mia could not eat well with any of them and, as a last resort, she was given a regular bottle and a regular nipple. Of all the choices, it worked best. She had enough tissue behind her upper gum line to be able to manage it. She did manage it, but with a lot of choking, coughing, and gagging. Feeding time became one of the most—if not *the* most—uncomfortable thing to endure during the first few days, weeks, and months of her life.

Our goal was for Mia to be able to take in 20 cc's, which is not even one ounce, in one feeding. When she accomplished that, we could take her home. She reminded me of a tiny bird, mouth wide open, trying desperately to receive nutrition from her mother. It was a long and arduous routine, each time feeling like little progress had been made, only to have to do it all over again in a couple of hours.

As much trauma as our child was having to endure, our experience in the NICU was much better than the situations many people go through, especially those whose infants face life-threatening circumstances. Still, Jase and I wanted to get her out of the NICU as soon as possible so we could get her home where she could be held and soothed as much as she needed, not merely a few times a day. I definitely needed to bond with my baby, and I knew she needed to bond with me, too.

Finally, on the sixth day of our hospital stay, Mia weighed five pounds, fourteen ounces, and had been able to take 20 cc's of nourishment. Woo-hoo! She was ready to go home!

A kind nurse snuck Mia into my room several hours before we were scheduled to leave the hospital. Prior to that day, only Jase and I, my parents, and Miss Kay had seen her. When word got out that Mia was with us, Alan and Lisa, along with Korie and her children, John Luke and Sadie, as well as Reed and Cole, all came to the hospital for the big reveal.

It was wonderful watching our boys and extended family members dote on our baby girl. Korie held Mia for a few minutes while all the kids checked her out, touching her little toes and playing with her hands. Korie told me later what had happened on her ride home from the hospital. When she asked her kids what they thought of Mia and her cleft lip, Sadie (who was about six at the time) replied, "There's something wrong with her lip?" She didn't even notice anything different. That was a huge encouragement and comfort to me. I had been apprehensive about how people would act or what they might say when they first saw Mia. I had no reason to be concerned. The way our family responded to Mia relieved my stress and anxiety.

The Robertsons are exceptional in the ways they embrace people and accept them as they are, and they relate to people in bighearted, open-minded ways. The way they dealt with Mia's situation was truly inspirational to me. When they saw Mia for the first time, they ooh-ed and ahh-ed over her as they would have over any other beautiful baby. They were genuinely excited about the new addition to the family, and they loved her instantly and completely. I could tell they were not trying to act a certain way toward her in order to console me or make me feel better. They were not gushing over her in ways that came across as phony or insincere. They meant every single one of the kind, encouraging words they spoke, and their happiness over her birth was deep and true.

No one tried to convince me that the challenges we faced with Mia were okay; everything about Mia *really was* okay with them. In fact, it was more than okay. They thought Mia was wonderful. I had observed these inspirational qualities of love and acceptance in the Robertsons for years, but that day my awareness and appreciation of their loving nature went to a whole new level.

At one point, the nurse came to check on us and was aghast when she saw all the people in the room! We were busted. She told us that everyone had to leave immediately. I knew we had broken the rules, but for me the chatter and excitement of our family were exactly the emotional boost I needed as we prepared to take Mia home.

After Jase left to take Reed and Cole home, my parents arrived with one of our friends. My mom and friend helped me dress Mia for the first time, a special moment for me. Her going-home outfit was the same one I had worn thirty-two years earlier when my parents took me home from the hospital—a dainty vintage dress with matching bottoms.

Home

I was so glad to get home with Mia. Both of us had been in the hospital for six stressful days, and I could not remember ever being so relieved to be back in the comfort of my own home, with my husband and all three of our children together under one roof. Jase and I knew our time at home would soon be interrupted by a trip that would last less than thirty-six hours, but would profoundly affect the rest of our lives.

On the day Mia was born, in the midst of the drama involving her wet lungs and her unexpected move to the NICU, I still remembered that we were supposed to call ICI in Dallas to let them know she had arrived. My primary mission at that time was to "get her fixed," to start the process of repairing the cleft as soon as possible. As I placed the call, I fully expected them to tell us to come to Dallas within a week, so I was surprised and disappointed when they asked us to wait seventeen days because Dr. Salyer was overseas.

We learned that every time he operated on a paying patient, he also did surgery on a child whose family did not have the means to compensate him. Typically, his gratis procedures took place outside the United States. When Mia was born, he was treating children in Germany. We admired what Dr. Salyer was doing for others, although waiting even a day longer was difficult for me.

As excited as Jase and I were to have Mia home, we were both nervous about caring for an infant with special needs. We remembered the night we brought Reed home from the hospital—neither of us slept because we had never had a baby before and were afraid something might happen to him. We wanted to be awake and alert if he needed us. With only six feet separating our two bedroom doors at the time, we heard every coo and cough Reed made.

One time during that first night, Reed sounded like he was choking. Jase flew out of bed and made it to Reed's crib in two leaps—quite a feat from a waterbed! There was absolutely nothing wrong with Reed. We were two brand-new parents learning how to adjust to caring for another living, breathing human being who was now entirely our responsibility.

Mia's situation was much different than Reed's, but Jase and I felt the same type of anxiety that accompanies bringing home a firstborn. Reed was born healthy in every way; she was born with certain challenges. Because Mia did not have the roof of her mouth, she had to be sitting straight up when she ate, which is not a natural position for a newborn! Once she had milk in her mouth, it often ran out her nose. Understandably, we were concerned about her breathing and choking, and about other functions involving the mouth and nose, such as swallowing. We learned to keep her head raised at all times, either holding her with her head up or placing her in her crib with a rolled blanket under the mattress to elevate it.

Eight years earlier, when Reed was born, I had bought a set

of cute little four-ounce bottles. Reed had such an appetite that those bottles became too small for him the day after we brought him home from the hospital. When Cole came along, I pulled out those bottles again, and it wasn't long before I had to switch to bigger ones. Before Mia was born, I thought the four-ounce bottles would be perfect for her, and I was excited about using them. But when she came home, those four-ounce bottles looked supersized to me. I could not imagine her taking a whole four ounces; our greatest hope was that she would simply drink one ounce per feeding.

Being able to feed her with a bottle at all, even one ounce at a time, was a remarkable accomplishment. Weeks earlier, when I had spoken with Sue at ICI, she had warned me that the hospital staff would most likely try to convince Jase and me to put Mia on a feeding tube soon after birth. "Don't do it," she advised us.

She explained that once babies begin to receive nourishment through a tube, they stop wanting to eat naturally, to the point that they almost give up. "Stand firm on this," she told us. "The hospital may say that a feeding tube is best for your baby, but it is not. An infant's nature is to suck, and your baby needs to suck, even though it will be difficult for her and she will have to work extra hard."

Sue knew what she was talking about. On the third day in the NICU, after seeing how little Mia was eating, the doctors strongly recommended inserting a feeding tube in her. We staunchly refused, hoping we were doing the right thing. That one piece of advice served us well. To this day, we are deeply grateful that someone shared that life-changing advice for our daughter with us. Even though feeding her made our first days at home quite difficult, we prayed about it, trusted God with it, and were able to do it.

Before Mia was born, I had planned to let her sleep in a bassinet in the master bedroom. When we brought her home, the bassinet was still in our living room, and we left it there. She spent much of her time in it, right in the middle of everything else going on in our home. In every way, she was the center of attention.

As we made our way anxiously and carefully through the next several days, we tried our best to prepare ourselves for the next phase of Mia's journey: our first trip to the International Craniofacial Institute. Because of the distance we had to travel, we decided to leave home the day before her appointments, spend the night with my brother and his family near Dallas, and then return home the following day after her appointments. Before we left we had no idea what our visit to ICI would hold. We simply knew Mia's future well-being depended on it.

▼ *All dressed up with Jase for junior prom*

▲ *With Miss Kay in the kitchen*

Our Beginning

▼ *Our wedding day*

▲ *Jase and me at his graduation from seminary. This was just twelve days before we got married!*

▲ *Reed and Cole are great brothers to each other.*

Early Years

◄ *Jase (still without his beard),*
Cole, me, and Reed at the beach

Just like their daddy! Reed and ►
Cole are ready to go hunting.

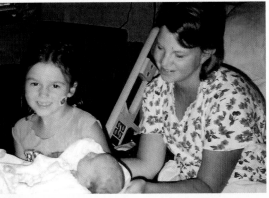

▼ *Cole gently giving his new baby sister a kiss*

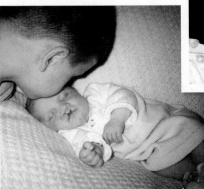

▲ *Sadie meets her newborn cousin Mia for the first time*

Building Our Family

◄ *Baby Mia dressed for her dedication*

My brave Mia after ► her second surgery. She takes the afghan Granny made for her into every surgery.

▼ Reed, Cole, and Mia acting silly with our dog, Daisy, as I try to take a photo of them

▲ Mia and Jase engaged in your typical father-daughter bonding activity

Family Fun

▲ A family day at the beach

Mia palling around with Uncle Willie, who ▶ lovingly nicknamed her "Mia Moo"—and it stuck

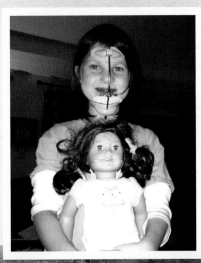

Mia worked hard to put in the necessary hours wearing her headgear. At least she had a friend to help her through it.

▲ *Mia holding hands with Reed as she walks out of the hospital only twenty-four hours after bone graft surgery*

Being Brave

▲ *Mia's friends surprised her by making beautiful snowflake decorations for her hospital room. Her cousins were there to hang them for her.*

▲ Mia and her cousin Bella cheering
on the high school football team

▼ Mia loves playing soccer and is extremely
competitive. I wonder where she got that from . . .

Living Life to the Fullest

◄ Mia giving her testimony at the
"She Speaks" event at Oklahoma
Christian University.

What's a little snow to a Robertson? ►
The kids with Daisy enjoying the outdoors.

▲ *Mia received an honorary service award in Washington, DC, presented by Congressman Trent Franks.*

In the Spotlight

Behind the scenes of the "Stand by Mia" ▶
episode: Jase, me, Mia, Korie, and
Jess watching Si and the kids wrestle

▲ *The entire Robertson clan gathers together for a family photo during the filming of*
"Stand by Mia." Mia asked for a family reunion, and she got one!

My support system (left to right): LinDee, me, Paula, Kim, Lisa, Bonny

I'm thankful for my parents (standing between me and Reed) whose faith greatly influenced my own.

Truly Blessed, Blessed... Blessed

Our family before Mia's distraction surgery—there for each other, as always, through thick and thin

After Mia's distraction surgery, friends and family filled her room with loving support.

6
Seventeen Days Old

WHEN MIA WAS SIXTEEN DAYS OLD, Jase and I piled into the car with her, my parents, and Miss Kay early in the morning and headed to ICI, located at Medical City Dallas. My aunt Bonny, who is like a big sister to me, drove from her home in Austin that night and met us at my brother's house so she could also accompany us.

The next morning, although we thought we had allowed plenty of time to reach the medical complex, we underestimated the Dallas traffic and ended up being forty-five minutes late. Because we had a full day of carefully scheduled appointments, I knew that being tardy for the first one would have a domino effect on the entire day. I am normally a punctual person, and being forty-five minutes behind schedule was a major stressor for me. Needless to say, the day did not get off to a peaceful start, and I was anxious before we even reached the parking lot of the medical facility.

Jase and I had not taken Mia anywhere after we left the hospital, so our trip to Dallas was her first outing. We packed everything we might need—an overloaded diaper bag, her bottles, blankets, baby carrier, stroller, and anything else we thought might make the day easier for her. Mia's entourage of family members all proved to be helpful and supportive to Jase and me on that difficult day. While we were meeting with various doctors, our family stayed in the waiting rooms of each office, meeting other patients and families who shared valuable information and inspirational stories about their journeys with craniofacial challenges. The moral support they received in those waiting rooms was amazing. Knowing our family, I'm confident they provided plenty of encouraging words to others as well.

We were scheduled to see each member of Mia's craniofacial team that day, starting with an orthodontist, whose office was not located within ICI, but a short drive away.

The Orthodontist

I was so flustered and apologetic about being late to our first appointment that all I could do was keep telling the receptionist in the office how sorry we were. Her smile and calm, reassuring manner immediately put me at ease as she said, "Mrs. Robertson, we have many out-of-state patients. We are sensitive to the fact that you have to drive a long distance to get here. It's not a problem. I'll let them know you are here, and I will also let the rest of the team know you will be running late to your other appointments today." Those compassionate, understanding words did quite a lot to relieve some unnecessary anxiety for this mama.

We saw the orthodontist first because he was responsible for making Mia's palatal appliance, a retainer-like piece (without the metal) that would fit around her top gum line and serve as an artificial palate (basically a removable barrier that would function as an interim roof for her mouth). She would wear it for seven months. The appliance takes several hours to make, so all new patients get the process under way early in the day to have it ready to pick up before they leave.

Jase and I had no idea how traumatic fitting a palatal appliance could be for an infant. We certainly did not expect it to be a pleasant experience for Mia, but it was much worse than we ever imagined. To accomplish the fitting, I sat in a chair with Mia on my knees and facing me. The doctor said, "We will have to put a mold in her mouth in order to get a fitting. She will scream bloody murder, but that's a good sign. If she's crying, it means she's breathing."

I thought, *Okay, crying is good. Remember, crying is good.*

Some of the orthodontics staff positioned themselves behind Mia and inserted the mold, similar to what happens when a dental impression is made. And Mia did scream bloody murder— like the orthodontist predicted. Knowing my daughter had a disability and then watching people make her suffer, even for a reason that would eventually help her, was gut wrenching for me, much more so than I had anticipated.

After about sixty seconds, the orthodontist removed the mold and said, "Okay, you can pick her up now and soothe her. The worst part is over." I already had Mia held to my chest by the time he finished talking, trying to comfort her and calm her down. "I'll be back in a couple of minutes after I check this mold."

Jase and I sat there patting and rubbing Mia's back. She was almost completely calm when the orthodontist came back in the room and said, "I'm sorry to tell you this, but the impression did not take. We have to do it again."

Whoa! I was not expecting that.

Jase looked at me and said, "I can't do this."

Speechless, I looked at him as if to say, *"What?"*

"I just can't watch that again," he said before he abruptly turned and walked out of the room.

I could hardly believe it. Jase, my rock, had left me all alone with our seventeen-day-old baby, who was about to endure again what must have been the most frightening, uncomfortable situation of her life. I was angry with him for leaving me to handle this by myself. But I had no choice. Both of us couldn't walk out.

I took a deep breath, laid Mia back down on my knees, and said, "Okay, let's do it."

I realized right then and there that I was going to have to be the one to handle the logistics of these appointments. I had no idea what exactly that meant at that moment, but I knew it was up to me to get Mia through each doctor's visit, keeping her as comfortable as possible, but with no excuses. If I wanted the best possible care and outcome for my daughter, I had to dig deep and get it done—which is exactly how I proceeded for the rest of the day.

I learned later that Jase had gone outside to the parking lot. He has always found solace, strength, and comfort in the outdoors—usually in a duck blind—if he has something to think or pray about or if his emotions threaten to get the best of him. He had been so angry that the molding process had to be redone that he was visualizing hitting the orthodontist between the eyes with his fist, which obviously would have made this whole ordeal much worse. So he left. There were no duck blinds in sight where he could pull himself together; the parking lot was as close to nature as he could get, and by the time he rejoined us, he was much better.

During the visit with the orthodontist, Mia not only had her mouth looked at extensively and sat through the poking and prodding necessary to start making the palatal appliance, she also had X-rays done on her mouth. There, in the gums, Mia had all of her teeth except for one, even though most of them were nowhere near being in the right places. I thanked God for the first bit of good news of the day.

We loaded up in our Suburban and drove the four miles to Medical City Dallas, where the rest of the craniofacial team was located. All the while I tried to reassure both sets of parents, Bonny, and Jase that Mia was okay. Other families and patients in the waiting room had heard Mia wailing from the treatment room, and everyone was emotional by the time we left.

As soon as we arrived at Medical City Dallas, I knew how the place had gotten its name. It really did seem like a small city to us: an enormous sprawling complex of buildings, offices, suites, hallways, and elevators. We were not prepared for the magnitude of it and the long distances we had to walk between doctors' offices.

ICI had sent us a detailed schedule before we left home, but even with that information, we found the buildings difficult to navigate. Thankfully, everyone we encountered was friendly, kind, and compassionate, and they all went out of their way to be helpful, happily pointing us in the right direction or escorting us to the places we needed to go. We eventually found our way to each office and soon discovered that wrapping our minds around the physical aspects of such a large medical facility was nothing compared to absorbing mentally and emotionally all that we were learning and watching our baby girl endure.

As we went from station to station, we came across other families whose children were patients at Medical City. Like us, they had their own personal support teams. Seeing so many suffering children with their own unique challenges was overwhelming. Realizing we were not alone—that there were families just like us, and that our little girl could have had much greater difficulties—gave us a sense of strength. At the same time, we felt guilty for never before reaching out to help families who were going through such hardship. It was a sad, surreal, eye-opening experience.

I overcame the shock of being in a place with so many suffering children by getting myself into "work mode." I was on a mission, and I had a list of tasks to complete. I did not allow the emotional burden of the day to influence me; I chose to remain strong, objective, and attentive to everyone we needed to meet and everything that was happening, true to my nature. Even though I became mentally overwhelmed by everything we learned about Mia's condition as the day wore on and was deeply touched when I saw tears in my husband's eyes when he reached his breaking point, I did not allow myself to lose focus or break down. I could not allow it. Mia needed me.

The Speech Therapist

Before our visit to the speech therapist, Dr. Elizabeth Sperry was little more than a name on a piece of paper to me. In fact, I wondered why we needed a speech therapy expert in the first place. Mia certainly did not have any speech to evaluate! At the same time, we began to realize that Mia was in for a long journey.

The moment we met Dr. Sperry, I knew our time with her was more than just another appointment. This kind, gracious woman thoroughly understood everything Mia would most likely face and all she would probably need for the foreseeable future. Her wealth of knowledge about the complicated process of helping cleft patients and their families would be invaluable, and she would eventually become the core of our entire experience at ICI.

At our first meeting, Dr. Sperry explained that her role in

Mia's journey would be to make sure our daughter was progressing as she should and hitting all the right milestones. In addition, she would be preparing us for surgery and making sure I knew how to care for Mia after her operations. Her gifts and responsibilities far exceeded the title of "speech therapist."

I was surprised when Dr. Sperry gave Mia a physical exam, first checking our baby's fingers and toes for any sign of a web. The doctor then began to look for signs of numerous other syndromes that can accompany cleft lip and palate. That was the first time we realized Mia could have other problems too; we had arrived that day thinking her lip and palate were our only concerns. We found out, though, that many children with cleft lip and palate do have other conditions, and that was both a shock and a source of anxiety.

Thankfully she said, "I can't see anything physically wrong with her, but the surgeon will do a more thorough evaluation." He was our next stop.

While our family members sat in Dr. Sperry's waiting room, they met and talked to the parents of a child about a year old who suffered from craniosynostosis. Her skull had fused together too early, so she was born without a soft spot, giving her brain nowhere to expand. Therefore, this sweet little baby girl was scheduled to have her skull cut open the next morning to allow her brain room to grow, thus giving her a chance at a better life. We heard stories like this all day long.

The Surgeon

We met Dr. Kenneth Salyer, the surgeon we firmly believed to be the best choice for our daughter, in yet another office suite in that vast medical complex. This office had hundreds of photographs filling the walls—pictures of children he had treated. "Wow," said Jase, "this guy's work looks better than anything we've seen."

I could tell by the clothing and hairstyles that some of the photos were quite dated, and I took that as a good sign. To me, it indicated that the doctor had operated at a high level of success for a long time. As we waited for him to enter the room, the images on the walls encouraged us.

Dr. Salyer was tall, with a shock of gray hair, and wore a tailored suit. A group of young doctors in white coats, participants in a fellowship at ICI, followed him into the room. His commanding presence set the tone of our short appointment. After examining Mia, he basically gave us a plan, told us what he would do, and let us know what we should expect:

> at three months old: repair lip
> at six to eight months old: repair palate
> before kindergarten: a single procedure to repair and touch up the lip/nose area (because there is not much to work with in that space at three months)
> just before adult teeth come in (at approximately seven years old): bone graft surgery

Jase and I had only one question once Dr. Salyer examined Mia and, like Dr. Sperry, found nothing additional to be concerned about. "Can we go ahead and schedule the surgery?"

"Before you leave today, you'll make an appointment for her, but she has to weigh at least twelve pounds in order for anesthesia to be administered," he said. With Mia weighing less than six pounds that day, I knew we were going to have to work even harder to get her the needed calories.

We gathered our things and headed to the next appointment. On our way, we tried to assimilate everything Dr. Salyer had said. I remembered bits and pieces: "We want her to look the best she can possibly look when she starts school. . . . We want her speech to be the best it can possibly be. Speech is very important to me. . . . A big surgery at about age seven . . . she'll have to go through physical therapy to help her walk again after that one because we take bone from her hip and graft it to the upper jaw. . . . We take things as they come. . . . Every child grows differently. . . ."

In my mind, the surgeon had laid out a road map for healing but also a road map for considerable trauma for many years. It was overwhelming; all I could do was focus on the first surgery. I heard the rest of what he had said, but I could not allow myself to start processing it. In addition to all the information fighting for my attention, as a budget-oriented person, I started seeing serious dollar signs after our visit. Jase and I had already committed to getting Mia the best care possible. We had talked through the financial ramifications of taking her to ICI. We were committed to it, but now reality was hitting me in a whole new way.

Out next stop was at a place the Institute simply called "media." For Mia and for us now, "media" means television and radio interviews, magazine photos, and other print material about our show or our family. But when Mia was an infant, the word referred to the large number of photographs taken at ICI to visually document each stage of an individual patient's medical progress. The media room was equipped with the highest definition cameras Jase and I had ever seen. We could not believe the clarity of the eight-by-ten-inch images they took. The walls of the room were decorated with various designs, such as stars or diamonds, and the photographers would tell the patients where to swivel and what to look at so that they could capture every possible angle of the patient's face or mouth. This place would become a very familiar environment over the next several years.

As we prepared to leave for our next appointment, the photographer noticed us looking at our map and trying to figure out exactly where to go. He offered to personally walk us to our next appointment—just another example of the patience and kindness that each caregiver extended to us that day. They treated us as though Mia were the only patient in the entire complex. She obviously wasn't, but that was the way everyone made us feel.

The ENT

By the time we saw Dr. Trone, the ear, nose, and throat specialist, my brain was on complete overload. Dr. Salyer had explained to us that whenever he operates on a new patient, he asks an ENT to put tubes in the patient's ears. Cole had suffered from ear infections as an infant, and when he was three years old, tubes were used to help him. However, we questioned the need for tubes in Mia's case because she had not had any ear infections since she was born. We simply did not want to do it if it wasn't necessary.

"Ninety-eight percent of all cleft babies have chronic ear infections," Dr. Salyer had explained. "If you go ahead and place the tubes in while she's under anesthesia, then you can be sure you won't have trouble with her ears." We saw the logic in that, so we signed the paperwork and authorized Dr. Trone to insert the tubes in Mia's ears during the lip repair surgery.

The Surgical Coordinator

Our last visit before returning to the orthodontist to pick up Mia's palatal appliance was with Dr. Salyer's surgical coordinator.

We were able to schedule Mia's first surgery for December 17, 2003, eight days before Christmas, on the condition that she weighed twelve pounds by then.

My Weak Moment

Our heads were nearly bursting with information by the time we reached the orthodontist's office to have Mia's palatal appliance fitted and learn its use. The visit started off okay, although all three of us—Mia, Jase, and myself—were exhausted after such a long day.

When the orthodontist had explained earlier that day that the appliance was "like a fake palate," he told us it would "help her eat better and keep things from going up her nose so easily." He did not tell us until we picked up the appliance that it had to be washed and reinstalled after every feeding.

"After *every* feeding?" I asked.

"Yes, ma'am," he answered.

"But she eats *eight times* a day," I said.

"Okay, then you'll need to remove it from her mouth, wash it, and reapply it eight times a day."

For some reason, that brief conversation completely threw me. It was the most devastating news I had heard all day. I already had so many extra things to do for Mia in addition to the normal care of an infant. And now I had to clean a palatal appliance eight times a day, reapply Fixodent, and press it back into my baby's mouth, keeping it in place until the Fixodent took hold? And it had to start that very day; she would leave the orthodontist's office with it in her little mouth. I could not take even a little breather after such a hard day of doctors' visits.

In the orthodontist's office that afternoon, I realized there was no going back on our journey. A new rhythm of life unfolded for me in that moment, and I found myself thinking, *I cannot manage one more thing, especially not something that has to be done eight times a day.* The thought of it crushed me at the end of such an intense day.

How am I going to do this? I thought, knowing the cleaning responsibility would fall on me. I left the orthodontist's office feeling totally spent, thankful to be headed home.

Back to West Monroe

I cannot remember a more exhausting day than the one we spent at Medical City that first time we visited. To this day, I can say that it was one of the most traumatic days I have ever endured. My heart goes out in a special way to every parent who has ever had to watch a son or daughter endure suffering for any reason, especially to those whose children face medical challenges.

Having several of our family members with us on the trip to Dallas was a blessing all day long. We were all emotionally drained, but I also had the added physical stress of having had a C-section two and a half weeks earlier. None of us knew how much we would be walking that day. In the car on the way home, my mom said, "I can't believe I didn't think about getting you a wheelchair today." Honestly, I never thought about it myself. My only concern that day was for Mia.

One of the unexpected joys of our ride home that evening was that my parents and Miss Kay were full of stories about people they had met in waiting rooms throughout the day. It seemed as though they encountered the people we needed to share with us their success stories, provide information and opinions on certain doctors, and talk about what to expect as Mia progressed on her journey. Since Jase and I did not meet most of those people, having our family members pass along so much encouraging information from these other journeyers lifted our weary spirits a bit and gave us hope for the future. We started to realize how blessed we were.

We arrived home between 11:00 p.m. and midnight, and after I made sure Mia and the boys were tucked in, I collapsed in bed and crumbled emotionally. Jase was silent. He did not want to talk about anything—the trip, the doctors, the road ahead of us—*anything.* I did want to talk—I *needed* to talk—but had no one to listen. I know now that Jase and I each have our own ways of dealing with things, and one is not better or worse than the other; our coping styles are just different. That night, I ended up dealing with the events of the day by sitting on the edge of our bed and sobbing for about half an hour before exhaustion finally overtook me. Jase simply went to sleep as soon as his head hit the pillow.

Step It Up

The following evening, after a day of settling into being at home with Mia and our new routine of dealing with her palatal appliance, I was caught off guard when Jase called eight-year-old Reed, five-year-old Cole, and me into the living room. I had no idea he had planned a family meeting with all of us and was shocked when I heard him say, "All right, boys. Here's the deal. We've just gotten back from Dallas, and we got some hard news. Mom is going to have to spend a lot of time taking care of Mia, so we're going to have to step it up around here. From now on, you will get yourselves up in the morning, get dressed without any help, eat your breakfast, brush your teeth, and get your back-packs ready for school."

I could hardly believe what I was hearing. They were little boys accustomed to my help with almost everything in the mornings! So I objected. "What? No, Jase. They don't have to do that. I can still do that. They are way too young to do all these things. This sounds crazy."

Jase said to me, "Oh, yeah. They can do it."

He calmly and matter-of-factly turned his attention to Reed and said, "Go get my alarm clock." Excitedly, Reed went, while Cole and I sat silently, looking at Jase. When Reed returned, Jase told him, "This is now *your* alarm clock. I'll teach you how to use it. When it goes off in the mornings, you are to get yourself out of bed and then get your brother up. And then you both need to do what I've talked to you about doing for yourselves."

Reed nodded his head vigorously and said, "I can do it, Dad."

"What is the first thing you are going to do when the alarm goes off?" Jase asked Reed.

"Get up and brush my teeth."

"Nope."

"Get up and get dressed?"

"Nope."

After a few seconds of intense thought, a light went on in Reed's eyes. "Get up and wake up Cole!"

"Yes!" Jase said. "Now y'all go get ready for bed."

When Jase finished talking to the boys and they had left the room, I looked at him with my mouth hanging open, stunned by what he had asked of our young sons. I did not feel good about this new arrangement at all because I was the mom, and I wanted to keep being the mom I had always been to Reed and Cole. I did not like the fact that Jase thought the new realities of our life needed to impact our established routine in such a drastic way.

"It won't work," I told him.

"Yes it will," said Jase. "Did you see how excited Reed was when he realized he has some new responsibilities? This is not only helping you, Missy, it's also giving them a sense of being able to contribute to our new challenge, to feel like they're helping the family."

The next morning, Reed and Cole did exactly what Jase had told them to do. Since that night, I have never had to wake them in the mornings. (Well, maybe a few times when they were teenagers and didn't want to get up!) My eight- and five-year-old boys took that task to heart. Jase was right.

Jase was sure his plan would work based on his own childhood experience. Several members of the Robertson family, including Jase, have written about the Robertson brothers' upbringing, and those stories are detailed in other books. I will simply say here that Alan, Jase, and Willie had to take care of themselves in many ways once they were old enough to do so, with Alan taking the lead. He would often do things parents did in other households, such as cooking, cleaning, and bathing his younger brothers.

By the time Jep came along, the family was much more stable, and Phil and Miss Kay were better able to take care of him. Jase is quick to say that as a boy, if he wanted to go to school, he had to get himself out of bed in the mornings and get ready to go. Maybe that's why when he told Reed and Cole what they needed to do, Jase knew they would rise to the challenge he gave them.

As anxious as I was about dealing with Mia's palatal appliance so many times a day, we settled into our routine, and I quickly mastered the frequent cleaning with dish soap and a toothbrush.

I eventually realized I did not have to clean it after every feeding, so I tried cleaning it thoroughly after every other feeding. Mia's gums were not becoming irritated and she was having no problems from less frequent cleanings, so I decided to save her the extra trauma of removing and inserting it so often, especially in the middle of the night when I was trying to get her on a normal sleep schedule.

I have been a rule follower all of my life, and I am normally so good about obeying doctors' orders that sometimes the doctors themselves are surprised that I have done everything they have recommended. But when it came to cleaning that appliance, I also knew that I had two other children and a husband who needed my care and attention, and that what I was doing was sufficient. It posed no problem whatsoever for Mia. Sometimes, things have to give a little bit in the interest of the greater good, especially in a family, and in this case, I made an executive decision. As I write this book, eleven years have passed without any ill effects.

Looking back to the night of the alarm clock, I see how wise Jase was in our family meeting. He has always been the kind of person who can think about things in silence, analyze them, pray about them, make decisions, and then execute a plan. He is wired that way. No matter what happens, Jase will not react to it, and he does not act hastily. He is not one to get caught up in the excitement of a moment or the intensity of certain circumstances. He observes the situation, ponders and prays, then does what needs to be done. I think about the way my husband and sons have loved and supported me as I have cared for Mia physically since we made that first trip to Dallas. And I think of the way they have loved and adored Mia, and I know that I am truly blessed.

7
New Realities

ONE OF THE BIGGEST emotional adjustments I had to make after our first trip to Dallas was embracing the truth about Mia's condition. I thought I had done a good job facing the realities of her cleft lip and palate, but once Jase and I listened to multiple doctors discuss numerous surgeries and talk about her still being in treatment five, ten, or twelve years from that day, the seriousness and the long-term ramifications of her situation really began to hit me.

Any time I hear about others who are experiencing circumstances similar to Mia's, one thing I want to share with those parents and families of children with special needs is that I went through a grieving process. I want others to know that grieving is healthy and normal, not something to be repressed or something to feel guilty about. Let me explain.

Even though no one had died, the grief I felt in the weeks and months after Mia's diagnosis was real. I was not grieving the loss of a *person*, but the loss of a *perception*—my perception of the perfect life. In my mind (and I know I am not alone in this), the "perfect" life was one in which I enjoyed a loving, happy marriage with my husband and with all my family members living relatively normal, healthy lives. My view of perfection did not include years of doctors' visits and one surgery after another. Until we went to Dallas, something deep inside of me, something I was not completely in touch with, kept holding out hope that for some reason our situation might not be as daunting as it appeared. Beneath the surface of my thoughts and emotions, there was a part of me that believed Mia might be spared some of the difficulties we had heard about. Who could blame me for that?

That long day at ICI forced me to face the new realities of our lives and required me to view the situation as one we would need to manage for years, not one that could be fixed in weeks or months. As the impact of this truth sank in and my denial subsided, I went through subsequent stages of grief until I reached a place of acceptance. This process took a while for me to get through, and I would never want to tell anyone how long it should take because everyone is unique, and every circumstance has its own dynamics.

Anyone who googles "stages of grief" will find lots of information, including Elisabeth Kübler-Ross's five stages of grief, as well as models that other people have developed—one that encompasses four stages of grief and another that includes seven. The point is not how many stages there are; rather that each person should grieve thoroughly and appropriately in his or her own way and not try to follow a specific program.

Most grief models end with "acceptance," but my personal journey of processing grief took me beyond acceptance to something even more powerful. I had an epiphany—a principle I knew intellectually suddenly became a deep conviction in my heart. I learned in a whole new way that what we view as perfection is not what God views as perfection. He sees us and our situations much differently than we do. From His perspective, not only was Mia perfect, our family's life and the plan He had for our future was perfect too.

Mia is extremely practical minded. She calls things as she sees them. The fact that her mouth is not what the world would view as perfect is not news to her, and she speaks openly about it. When Mia was born, her challenges were completely unexpected. I could not have predicted them and would not have wished them for her, but I have learned that the fact that I am not in control is clearly a good thing! I cannot imagine my life without this child, exactly the way she is.

Getting to Know Her

The two and a half months between Mia's first visit to ICI and her first surgery to repair the cleft in her lip were an amazing gift to me. I quickly realized that having a baby girl was totally different from having boys, and I was thankful for the chance to experience both. I enjoyed seeing glimpses of her personality, playful and strong, and recognizing her likes and dislikes. I loved rocking her, singing to her, and feeding her. Some of my longtime dreams began to come true during that ten-week period—dressing Mia in beautiful clothes with frilly socks, cute shoes, and plenty of pretty hair bows. Those days were special and fun. I knew we had a surgery ahead of us, but I chose not to focus solely on that but to savor each happy day with my baby girl.

Because I was relatively certain that Mia would be my last baby, even 2 a.m. feedings were special to me, something that I did *not* see as a delight with the boys. I trained each of my children to sleep through the night at a young age—Reed by six weeks, Cole by seven weeks, and Mia at four weeks, thanks to the head start the nurses in the NICU had given her with their rigid schedule. I knew these middle-of-the-night feedings would not last long, and I decided to enjoy them while I had them. Those moments became very special—spending that time with her, just the two of us in the dark and quiet, while I watched and listened to her suck, swallow, and breathe, all while I softly sang songs about how much God loved her.

When Mia came home from the hospital, Reed and Cole were typical boys accustomed to running through the house, having brotherly quarrels, and playing in their rough-and-tumble way. Their behaviors did not change after Mia joined our family; they remained "all boy." But I noticed that both of them were extremely gentle and tender toward her. When they came home from school every afternoon, they were quick to run to her bassinet and check on her, stroking her tiny hand or speaking softly to her. Those interactions never lasted very long and soon gave way to typical boyish play, but I will always treasure the way Mia's big brothers felt about her and acted toward her in those early days. I could tell that she really meant a lot to them. They truly loved her, and they still do.

Mia Goes to Church

Jase has always been a little paranoid about germs. I know, that seems odd for someone who hunts and dresses animals for a living. But it's true. He will not give a second thought to skinning a deer in our driveway or cleaning frogs in our living room, but he is very careful about things like washing his hands after being in public places and shaking hands with people, as well as drinking from public water fountains. I call him a "germaphobe," and his biggest germ phobias were evident when Mia was an infant. I have to admit that I became germaphobic, too, during those first few months of her life. I did not want anything to delay her lip repair operation.

Jase and I were extremely anxious about taking Mia to church for the first time, not only because of all the germs we knew she would be exposed to from the number of people she would en-counter, but also because our church family knew she would look different from other babies. We knew many people were curious about her, and we were nervous about how they would respond to her.

Korie's sister, Ashley, was one of the first people we saw after we gingerly carried Mia into the church building that day. She relieved my apprehension immediately when she walked up to me, eager to see the baby, and said, "Missy, she is so cute!"

Her comment seems so genuine, I thought. I knew she was sin-cere, and I was slightly surprised to find that I believed her.

"Thank you," I said, thinking, *Wow. She really meant that.*

Some of our fellow church members seemed to know what to say to put me at ease, and Mia's first Sunday at church turned out to be easier than I had expected. Jase and I felt our congregation's love and support that day, and when it was over we were thankful for compassionate friends who loved us, loved our boys, and now loved Mia unconditionally.

After we had taken Mia to church, I felt a little better about taking her other places, but I knew that people in the general public were not likely to be nearly as sensitive and kind as the people at our church. When I first started taking Mia out, I often pulled up the canopy on her car seat so people would not stare at her and ask questions.

When Mia was born, I felt her cleft defined who she was, and I offered an explanation to people before they asked, simply be-cause I didn't want to wait for the inevitable "What's wrong with her?" question I was certain would always follow after that first glance. In actuality, this has happened only once in her lifetime.

One day in a grocery store, a man walked up to Mia and me and made quite an effort to see her, almost sticking his head inside her car seat. The inappropriateness of his actions bothered me instantly.

"What's wrong with her?" he asked.

"She was born with a cleft lip," I responded curtly.

"What's that?" he asked.

"It's when a baby's lip doesn't develop as it's supposed to during pregnancy," I answered as calmly as possible, upset with his rudeness.

"Huh?" he said.

I tried my best to explain, but I wanted to get us away from his prying eyes and annoying questions.

As I reflected on that incident later that day, I realized that the one scenario I had been trying so hard to avoid had happened. As awkward as it was for me, I decided maybe it had happened for a reason—to force me to deal with a difficult question. *Was I really trying to shield Mia from curious people?* I wondered. *Was I trying to protect her—or was I trying to protect myself?*

We've Been Robbed!

As the time for Mia's surgery drew near, one of the events we were most looking forward to was her baby blessing, a time of celebration, prayer, and dedication for new babies and their families in our church. This occasion is also a time when parents receive a charge and make a promise to instill God's Word in their children. The parents also receive a new Bible for their child—pink for girls and blue for boys. Mia's baby blessing was scheduled for the Sunday before her first surgery.

Everything seemed normal when I picked up the boys and their cousin, Will, from school the Friday before that special service. We got home and the boys piled out of the car, ran into our house, and started playing. I got Mia out of the car and walked toward the house carrying her in her carrier, along with a couple of bags of groceries. With my hands full, I walked through the door from our carport into our house and kicked it closed behind me. It didn't close, but bounced back toward me. That's when I realized that the doorframe was mangled, and the door was bent. I looked at it thinking, *Did an animal do that?* Then it hit me—someone had broken into our house.

Since it was just a few weeks before Christmas, I quickly glanced at our tree, surrounded by wrapped gifts. All the presents seemed to be there. *Could the robber still be in the house?* I didn't want to scare the boys, so I calmly corralled them back into the car and drove next door to Mac's house, where I quietly told him what I had discovered.

"Call Jase," Mac instructed me, "and call the police." He grabbed a gun and said, "I'll go check things out."

Soon, Mac returned and told me that he hadn't found anyone inside. The police came, looked around our house, fingerprinted various surfaces, and ultimately surmised that the perpetrators were probably teenagers.

When we were able to take an inventory of what was missing, we realized only a few things had been stolen—the boys' Nintendo and all of their Nintendo games, some DVDs, and, worst for me, Mia's extra diaper bag, which I suppose the thieves used to carry their stolen goods. I had a diaper bag I carried with us when Mia and I went out for short periods of time, but I had another one with extra clothes and extra Fixodent for her palatal appliance. We did not lose anything of great monetary value, but we felt invaded, exposed, and vulnerable in ways we had never felt before.

Because we were going to Dallas for Mia's surgery a few days later, we did not have time to get the door fixed properly. Thankfully, Mac finagled it to a point where it would lock. The funny thing is that the door wasn't locked in the first place. Jase grew up in a home where the doors were never locked, and he never saw any reason for us to lock ours. "A locked door won't stop a thief," he reasoned, "so you might as well save your door." Those teenagers could have turned the handle! Now, since *Duck Dynasty* came into our lives, all of us Robertsons have learned to lock our doors. Better yet, we have installed high-tech security systems.

The day of the robbery was a day of drama, and it was certainly a time-consuming inconvenience, but all of us were safe. We did not lose anything expensive, irreplaceable, or sentimental. We lost our peace and sense of security temporarily, but we soon got past it and once again looked forward to Mia's baby blessing, two days away.

A Baby Blessing

Everyone in our family was excited about Mia's baby blessing the Sunday before we went to Dallas. Jessica, who is a wonderful seamstress, sewed a beautiful gown for Mia to wear that day. It was white with hand smocking on the front and resembled a very expensive christening gown. Mia also wore a bonnet and hand-crocheted booties that had been mine when I was a baby.

In our church, baby blessings precede the regular service. That morning Jase, the boys, Mia, and I stood up front surrounded by all of our family while the elders of our church prayed over us. During the baby blessing, the congregation always sings a song, which we call "the baby blessing song," a musical prayer asking for blessings on the baby, God's favor on his or her family, and a great future and godly legacy for the child. As we sing the song, we also watch a slide show featuring over-the-top adorable photos of the baby and the family. The pictures and the song are a sweet, special, joyous time for everyone there, often accompanied by clapping and laughter.

Our photos were beyond adorable, too, but I was aware that Mia's slide show wasn't typical for our church. While people were very kind and supportive, I knew they noticed that something was clearly different about her face. Unlike the other slide shows we had watched over the years, Jase and I heard no clapping, no happy giggles, no oohs and aahs. In fact, Jase clearly remembers hearing sniffles throughout the audience as the photos appeared on the screen. I did not notice sniffles, but I was aware that the mood in the church was unusually somber.

Although Mia's baby blessing was not like others, it was still a special time for our family. Even though her photographs were noticeably different from those of other babies, our family and friends still recognized the strength and beauty of this special little girl.

. . . And a Family Blessing

Later on in the service, Alan mentioned Mia's upcoming surgery as well as the break-in at our house. I could tell that people were furious on our behalf. Part of having a church family is that the people who love you really do rejoice when you rejoice and grieve when you grieve (see Romans 12:15). They also get angry when something unjust happens to you!

After the church service that day, a couple whom Jase and I did not know well approached us and gave us two hundred dollars—an enormous gift, in our minds. "Use it for travel, diapers, food—whatever you need," they said.

No one had ever done that kind of thing for us before, especially people we hardly knew. Their gift was a lot of money to us, enough to help cover two nights in a hotel, our meals, and our gas back and forth to Dallas. Their generosity covered most of our travel expenses, and we were surprised and grateful to be on the receiving end of such kindness.

But that wasn't all. Alan had mentioned to the congregation the types of items that had been stolen from us, and by Sunday evening the boys had some new Nintendo games, we had a new stash of movies, and there even was a new diaper bag for Mia. In those days, we did not have extra money to buy things like DVDs. Because of people's selfless giving, we ended up with more than we had to begin with! I estimate that we had twelve to fifteen movies before the robbery, but we had forty or fifty afterward.

Of all the things we lost, the diaper bag was the biggest loss for me because, as most moms understand, there are so-so diaper bags that do not function as well as they should; there are decent diaper bags; and there are *great* diaper bags. For me, the one that was stolen was a fabulous diaper bag. I had received it as a gift, and the woman who gave me the original one showed up at my house before we left for Dallas with an exact replacement. I have never forgotten that, and I will always appreciate it.

Our family was not in dire need of anything, that's for sure. But Jase and I were so touched by people's support. From the two-hundred-dollar monetary gift to each individual movie, we realized how much we were loved and how eager people were to encourage us and help us. Many of them did not know what to do or say about Mia's condition, but when they realized they could demonstrate their friendship through something as simple as replacing a stolen DVD, they rushed to do it.

Those expressions of support meant a lot to us, and now whenever I encounter people who want to know how they can help a family with a special-needs child or a child facing an illness, I tell them to do what they can do. If they are not sure what to say or how to support struggling parents, then take them a meal, provide some financial support through a monetary gift or a gift card, or give them a movie. Just do something to let them know you are thinking about them. Gestures that may seem small to the person who offers them can send great big messages of care and support to those who receive them.

A Great-Grandmother's Gift of Love

En route to Dallas, we decided to make a special stop in Arcadia, Louisiana, to introduce Mia to Jase's paternal grandmother. By that time, Jase's grandfather, Pa, had passed away, and Granny lived with Phil's older sister, Judy, in Arcadia. Jase had been particularly close to his grandparents, and since Granny had never seen Mia, this was the perfect opportunity.

Granny was a straightforward, matter-of-fact type of woman. I cannot remember ever seeing her cry or show much emotion, and she certainly was not the kind of great-grandmother who doted on babies, patted them gently, or cooed in their faces when she saw them. I wanted her to see Mia, but I wasn't expecting what happened when we got there.

A few minutes after we arrived, she asked Jase and me to come into her bedroom with her. As soon as she closed the door behind us, she said, "Do you need any money for this trip?"

I was shocked. Although I had known Granny for sixteen years, this was the most personal encounter I had ever had with her. Jase and I knew her finances were extremely limited, and in a mixture of being stunned by her offer and humbled by her love, we stuttered, "No, ma'am. Thank you very much, but we are fine."

Even with the two hundred dollars Jase and I had received from the couple at church, medical travel is expensive, and we could have used Granny's gift either on that trip or toward Mia's future expenses. But there was no way we were going to take money from Granny. We knew her offer was serious, and that gesture meant so much to us. It showed us how much she really cared about us in a way we had never seen before.

Before we left that day, Granny presented Mia with a special gift that she had made—a warm, beautiful afghan. Mia cuddled up with the soft blanket immediately. She soon started sleeping with it every night and has taken it into every single one of her surgeries thus far. The afghan is now faded and frayed, but Mia still sleeps with this physical reminder of Granny's love for us and makes sure it is packed for every trip we take.

Loving That Face

After our visit with Granny and Judy, we arrived at Medical City Dallas both nervous about the surgery and ready to put it behind us. As the preoperative processes began, I prayed that Mia would weigh enough to undergo surgery. For the previous two and a half months, I had worked hard to keep her weight up and had regularly taken her to the pediatrician to be weighed. I knew she would be very close to the required weight. The scale registered eleven pounds, five ounces, which was a few ounces shy of where she needed to be. Thankfully, the medical team deemed her weight acceptable. We were given a green light for surgery!

In the pre-op area I noticed a Christmas tree decorated with all kinds of stuffed teddy bears. The bears were in various colors and came with different types of accessories. As I was looking at the tree, a nurse came over and told me that the bears were for patients. "You can pick out one for Mia," she said. As I searched the tree for the right bear, the nurse reached around to the back of the tree and pulled out a bear with a green-and-cream-checkered bow—it was perfect.

Knowing that someone was thoughtful enough to care about patients and families facing surgery during the holidays meant so much to me. I loved the fact that Mia had a new teddy bear for her big day. Even now, Mia makes a great effort to pick out the right stuffed "friend" to take to the hospital with her.

The day of Mia's first surgery was not only a big day for her; it was a big day for me, too. Handing my three-month-old daughter to the anesthesiologist and watching her walk away with my baby was one of the most heart-wrenching things I have ever done. I knew that Mia was in someone else's care and that I had absolutely no control over what happened to her until after the procedure. I tried my hardest not to cry, but after the anesthesiologist walked through the secure doors, I broke down in Jase's arms. He was very emotional about the situation, too, but the two of us handled our intense feelings in different ways. I went to join our family in a large foyer area, where about fifteen of them had gathered to support us, and Jase headed outside to a small grove of trees near the parking lot.

As I mentioned earlier, being outdoors makes Jase feel closer to the Creator, who he knows can do mighty things. That grove of trees, which was surrounded by such a large concrete jungle, became a special place for Jase, a place where he said many heartfelt prayers.

The medical team had told us surgery would not begin until an hour or an hour and a half after the anesthesiologist took Mia back and that the procedure itself would last about an hour. They showed us to a small waiting room, one that was windowless and not nearly large enough for our family. When Jase composed himself enough to come back into the hospital, he met me there, but then we decided to leave and visit with our family in another area of the hospital.

We knew when Mia's surgery started, and we watched the clock as the hour passed. When it got close, Jase and I returned to the small waiting room. A full hour went by, then another fifteen minutes, then another fifteen minutes, and then another. After about an hour and forty-five minutes had passed, someone finally came in and told us the procedure went well.

"Dr. Salyer is very pleased with the operation," she said. "You can come back to the recovery room and see your baby."

During Mia's first visit to the ICI, the doctors had warned us that she would look different after her first surgery. I did not take that warning nearly as seriously as I should have because I thought, *That's the goal, isn't it—to make her look different?*

Actually, the ultimate goal of Mia's surgeries was to give her the proper foundation for quality breathing, eating, and speaking, but a successful by-product would be her new, forever-changing look. After the procedure, she did look different—*very* different. The minute I laid eyes on her, I no longer saw the face I had grown accustomed to since she was born. I had to remind myself that a different look was indeed our goal and that with this successful procedure, we had taken a big step in that direction.

Still, Jase and I were not at all prepared for the dramatic changes to Mia's face. She had railroad-track stitches running bilaterally from the base of her nose to her upper lip, and her entire face was swollen. None of the parents we had met whose children had already undergone the procedure had forewarned us. In fact, one mother later told me, "It's so shocking I did not know how to warn you. I just couldn't bring myself to tell you about it." I was frustrated at the lack of a heads-up on this. Now when Jase and I talk to parents of babies born with a cleft lip or palate, we do our very best to help prepare them for the drastic visual effects of the first surgery.

In the recovery room, Jase was trying to regain his composure, and I was crying, while our baby girl was lying there, looking miserable as she was trying to wake up from the anesthesia. Those moments were so traumatizing and dramatic for me—like nothing we had experienced before or since. I kept thinking about all of our family and friends who were waiting in the hospital foyer, wondering how the surgery had gone, but neither one of us could bear to face them.

After quite some time, when Jase was finally able to speak, he said, "We screwed up. We should have left her the way she was."

That was *not* what I needed to hear.

The sympathetic recovery nurse told us that Mia's face was swollen due to the procedure itself and that the swelling would go down in a couple of days. You would think that we would have realized that, but it wasn't sinking in. As much as we were counting the days until her face got "fixed," we had fallen deeply in love with that little face, cleft and all, and she had become not just "our daughter with a cleft." She had become our daughter. Period. No labels. No explanations. Just our daughter. And we loved her exactly the way she had been born.

The nurse gave us so much comfort that day. After she spoke

with us, Jase and I talked together and concluded that we could not have left Mia the way she was—the procedure was necessary to ensure her quality of life. Jase left to update the family while I held Mia. I felt deflated, and as I looked at Mia's stitched and swollen little face, I knew we were just starting out on this long and daunting journey—one that *must* be led by our faith and trust in God's care for us.

8
Learning Curves

WHEN YOUR FAMILY SELLS duck calls for a living, as ours did when Mia was an infant, sales meetings are extremely important—especially meetings with big clients. Jase's annual meeting with the buyer from Wal-Mart was scheduled for the day after Mia's surgery. He would present the new duck calls and hunting DVD, and ideally the Wal-Mart buyer would place a huge order for the upcoming year. The meeting had been scheduled weeks in advance, and we knew we could not miss it. I had prepared the samples and the sales presentation before we left for Dallas, so everything was ready.

Our plan before Mia's surgery had been for Jase to drive to the meeting after Mia was out of recovery and settled in her hospital room. The plan seemed perfectly reasonable to us when we came up with it. But then we saw Mia after her operation.

"I cannot leave," Jase said.

Even though my heart could not stand the idea of his leaving, I knew in my head that Jase had no choice.

"You have to go," I said firmly.

"I cannot leave," he repeated.

We talked about the situation and thought through our options. We knew Phil was busy with other commitments, and Willie and Korie did not work for Duck Commander at the time. There was absolutely no one else who could make the presentation. Jase had to go. Our entire livelihood, plus Miss Kay's and Phil's, basically depended on that one meeting. Miss Kay, always selfless and generous, immediately insisted that she go with Jase. Knowing my parents were at the hospital with me, and wanting desperately for someone to be at Jase's side to comfort and reassure him, I persuaded Jase to take his mom up on her offer. With a heavy heart, he left the hospital with Miss Kay and headed to Arkansas.

Bad Night, Good Recovery

My mom stayed with Mia and me in the hospital room that night. It was one of the most miserable nights I have ever lived through. Not only did I miss Jase, but we found out that Mia does not tolerate anesthesia well. She vomited most of the night and into the following day. Our expected one-night hospital stay became a two-night stay.

After being in the hospital for two days, the doctors released Mia to go home. The hospital sent us home with three things that proved helpful in her continued recovery. First, they gave us a wound-cleaning solution, which I applied with a cotton swab two or three times a day to the area where they had operated. I was diligent to keep that area clean, knowing cleanliness would facilitate the healing process.

In addition, the hospital gave us immobilizers called No-Nos, which were intended to prevent Mia from bending her arms and touching her mouth. These soft wraps are stiff on the underside, fasten easily with Velcro, and come in all sorts of cute colors and designs. Mia needed to wear these twenty-four hours a day for three weeks.

The hospital also gave us a special bottle—a soft bottle with tubing coming out of it—that the nurse taught me how to use. The tubing rests on the bottom lip, and the formula is slowly squeezed through the tube into the baby's mouth. Nothing about the bottle was difficult; it was just different and required some practice using it. Mia adjusted quickly, and so did I, which meant feeding her after surgery was never a big problem.

A week later, we returned to Dallas so Mia could have her stitches removed, again under anesthesia. Once the stitches came out, we began a whole new process involving a special kind of flesh-colored tape that needed to be applied to Mia's upper lip after her surgery to repair the cleft. This tape stretched the skin above the lip to prevent excessive scar tissue from forming. The medical staff told me to cut about a two-inch piece of tape, place it in the center above Mia's upper lip, and then press firmly on it from the middle to the edges. The goal was to flatten the area where scarring could occur as much as possible.

I'll admit that I wasn't keen about doing this; I can't imagine any mother wanting to tape her baby's lip. But I also had seen firsthand the appearance of other children's lips when the tape was used and when it was not. Without the tape, a child's upper lip tends to heal with more scar tissue than necessary, causing it to look thick and heavy. In contrast, when the tape is used, the lip typically heals and appears quite normal. I made up my mind that we would use the tape.

I understand the concern of having to keep tape on your baby's lip twenty-four hours a day, seven days a week—it draws attention to your baby and prompts questions from onlookers, but I urge parents to do it. It's a difficult but necessary part of the journey toward the ultimate goal of repairing the cosmetic effects of a cleft. I know that being diligent about the tape is not easy. I did it, though, and Mia has never had any scar tissue in the area where her cleft lip was repaired.

After making it through Mia's first surgery, we were so happy to get home from the hospital in time for Christmas. For years, my family had gathered at my aunt Bonny's house in Austin, Texas, around New Year's. Our family knew we could not travel so soon after Mia's surgery, so everyone converged at our house for a joyous holiday celebration.

Mia was recovering well—smiling, eating, gaining weight, and playing. Her eyes were bright, and her cheeks were rosy. Almost all day every day she had family members loving on her. We did not have to put the No-Nos on her, except at night, because she had not yet found her mouth! She was thriving, and I was thrilled. That Christmas was such a special, happy time for us. I knew that once the holidays were over, we would have to turn our focus to Mia's next surgery, four months away. But for the time being, I felt abundantly blessed to see her doing well after her first operation and to be surrounded by so many people who loved her and loved us.

Surgery at Seven Months

Mia recovered fully from her first surgery without complications, and once the recovery was behind her, we began preparing for the next procedure to correct her palate. Thankfully, our days of dealing with the palatal appliance would soon be over.

By the time Mia was ready for her next surgery, she had become as adept at flipping her palatal appliance out of her mouth as a teenager who flips a retainer. In fact, one Sunday we got home from church and discovered it wasn't in Mia's mouth, only to have Alan and Lisa's daughter Anna call to say that she had found Mia's palatal appliance in the church parking lot! That was an expensive piece of equipment, so we were glad the person who found it knew what it was and whom it belonged to.

As unhappy as I was about the palatal appliance when we first got it, it had proven to be helpful, as the orthodontist promised. But I was ready for Mia's palate to be closed, knowing the operation would be a huge step toward improving her quality of life. The day before her scheduled surgery was like a replay of the day before her first procedure. We packed the car and headed for Dallas.

By the time children are six or seven months old, they can be a little bit clingy, not wanting to let go of their mothers. The anesthesiologist gave Mia some "goofy juice," a calming sedative in a flavored drink, to relax her before taking her into the surgical suite, and it definitely worked. She was completely relaxed by the time they took her back. The medical team did pump her stomach before administering anesthesia, and they gave her antinausea medicine—lessons learned from her previous experience when she had gotten so sick.

I, on the other hand, fell into Jase's arms in a replay of what had happened when the doctor took her back for her first surgery. All I could think was, *I can't believe we're doing this again so soon.* I had really tried to psych myself up for that moment, telling myself repeatedly, "I got this. I've done this before. I'm going to be okay." Nevertheless, letting your baby go into an operating room to be put under anesthetic and have an operation is no small thing. It is an emotional event, and while I find that some surgeries are more emotional than others, I have learned to give in to the emotions.

With this particular surgery, part of the trauma for me was knowing how the procedure would be accomplished. The palate is made of cartilage—not bone. The front part of it is hard, and the back part is soft. Some surgeons choose to repair each part separately, but thankfully, the surgeons at ICI had learned to do it all at the same time, thus preventing further and unnecessary stress to the baby. To repair the hole in Mia's palate, where the roof of her mouth should have been, the surgeon would cut along the upper gum line on each side, pull the palate together, and sew it closed in the middle. Instead of a large hole in the center of the top of her mouth, Mia would now have holes on each side, along the gum line. Because of the amazing way God made the human body, the body recognizes the injury and begins to heal itself.

Thankfully, Mia was able to avoid what some children go through—the insertion of a nasal stent. I was aware of babies who had needed the stent because their nasal passages had collapsed. When there is no roof of the mouth, there is nothing for the nose to rest on. I could only imagine how uncomfortable a nasal stent would be and was relieved that Mia did not need it. All in all, the procedure went smoothly. The hospital had told us to plan for a two-night inpatient stay, but Mia recovered so well that we were able to leave after one night.

The day after her operation, the hospital sent us home with Tylenol and codeine. Over the next several days and weeks, I had to learn to read my daughter in new ways—her facial expressions, her gestures, the sounds of her cries. She could not tell me what she needed or how she felt, so I had to figure it out, which enabled me to understand who she is in much deeper ways.

Three or four days after surgery, I could tell Mia was really improving and feeling better. She looked good, but more than that, I could see her becoming a happy baby. She had not been unhappy before, but her level of joy and alertness seemed to rise day by day, and that was extremely encouraging to me. Within a week of her surgery, I dressed her up and took her outside for a few photographs. That entire season of our lives was good—beautiful spring weather, everyone in our family doing well, and a baby on the road to greater health. Within several weeks after surgery, Mia had graduated from the tube-feeding bottle to a regular bottle and then to baby food! She was able to eat like most other babies her age, and she was happy, happy, happy—as long as she was with me.

I was not accustomed to having a mama's girl or actually any kind of mama's baby. Both of my boys had been quick to let other people hold them or to play on their own without needing me with them. Not Mia. She was a mama's girl to the umpteenth degree. Anytime I tried to let someone else take her for a few minutes, she screamed like crazy until I took her back into my arms. If I was in her sight, it didn't matter who was around, including Jase—she wanted me. This was not easy because I had a full-time job at the time. Eventually I put a crib and some toys in my office at Duck Commander, but being so needed all the time wore me down. I suppose in Mia's mind she considered me an extension of herself because I was with her around the clock and tended to all of her physical and medical needs. I would say to other moms in a similar position that it's okay to admit how exhausting that kind of situation can be.

Her Needs Change

When Mia was close to a year old and fully recovered from her palatal surgery, I knew her dependency on me had to be dealt with. It was not good for her or for me. I needed some normalcy in my life, and she needed some too. The only problem was that I had a frame of reference for normalcy, and Mia did not. Her entire short life had been traumatic. Her demeanor was different than her brothers' had been. She was fussier and more easily agitated, and she did not sleep as soundly as the boys.

Mia also suffered from an unusual sensitivity to loud noises. When I asked the doctor about that, he said, "Remember, she was born with a crater in her head. It may be that sounds are magnified or that they reverberate in a way that bothers her." With our family's lifestyle, that became a challenge—not a big one, but still a frustration. When we went to Reed's and Cole's baseball games and the crowd started cheering, Mia would scream and then cry for about half an hour while I held my hands over her ears. Funny, her own loud screaming did not affect her; she was only bothered by the exuberant sounds of other people. Not surprisingly, the noise from fireworks bothered her, but oddly, and thankfully, she was perfectly happy when the sound of a duck call interrupted the quiet of an otherwise peaceful moment for her. I guess that's her Robertson genes!

Once Mia recovered from her palatal surgery, she did not need such dedicated care anymore. There were no stitches to clean, and there was no appliance to work with. Her next surgery was years away, and we could actually begin treating her as a typical growing baby. I understood that, but at less than a year old, Mia could not understand that. She and I both knew that I had been consumed with her for months, and she kept wanting to live with the same level of attention she had always been shown due to her needs. But those special needs no longer existed. She had the needs any baby her age would have—no more and no less—so I began to see her as a normal baby who needed to act in normal ways.

The problem with acting normal was that she had no idea what that meant. So I enrolled her in a local church's "Mother's

Day Out" program two days a week. She spent five hours there on each of those days, giving us both a bit of much-needed independence. This was a good break for me, and it was important in Mia's social development. After a few consistent days, she was absolutely fine with everyone there.

At that time in the Robertson family, Mia had several cousins her age. Willie and Korie's daughter Bella is a year older than Mia. Jep and Jessica's daughter Lily is nine months older, and their daughter Merritt is ten months younger. Those three cousins were built-in friends for Mia. Once she was able to play and interact like any other child, she got to know them and they got to know her. Those four little girls spent a lot of time together and formed a close bond that they still share.

A Speech Evaluation at Fifteen Months

As part of Mia's treatment plan, one of her checkups at ICI included an evaluation with Dr. Sperry, the speech therapist, when she was fifteen months old. I was shocked and disappointed when Dr. Sperry told me that Mia's speech was comparable to that of a child six to nine months old.

Before that day, my only experience with a speech therapy evaluation was when Melissa lived with us. Reed was two years and five months old at the time, and I was pregnant with Cole. For one of her speech therapy assignments, Melissa was supposed to conduct and record a thirty-minute conversation with a child who was two and a half to four years old and analyze it afterward. Reed was close enough to the required age, so one day she took him on a walk near our house and recorded their conversation. When she analyzed his speech, all she could say was, "I didn't do this right. This result is not possible."

Melissa took the results of her analysis to her professor, who echoed her opinion. "No, you did not do this correctly," she said. "Let me try it."

The professor's analysis showed the same results as Melissa's. At two years and five months of age, Reed's speech was on par with a child of four years and four months, almost twice his age! We all considered him very articulate, but we had no idea his speech was so advanced. I knew I was headed for trouble!

When Cole was around two years old, his speech was also advanced for his age; he was speaking in clear and complete sentences, while most of his little friends were still mostly pointing and gesturing. With two boys who excelled verbally, I was understandably upset to learn that Mia's speech was delayed. The therapist reassured me, saying, "It's okay. She needs some therapy, and she should be fine."

We learned about a program through Easter Seals in which a therapist visits children in their homes. Mia's therapist worked with her once a week, and she progressed very quickly. Within a few months, her speech was completely up-to-date and she was learning to form all her words and letters correctly.

Just a Regular Family—and Thankful for It!

The long reprieve before Mia's next surgery when she was five years old was a welcome relief. I felt that we became a "normal" family, like the other young families we knew. Jase and I enjoyed all the fun and responsibilities of having three children. The boys did well at school; we were active in church, as always; and we went to ball games and school performances and community activities. Mia was developing well, and I loved dressing her up and taking her places.

The only reminders of Mia's condition and the surgeries that would await her in the future were her regularly scheduled check-ups at ICI, which required a trip to Dallas once every few months, two sweet little white scars above her upper lip, and her medical bills. Even though ICI was out-of-network for our insurance company, they offered to write off a portion of Mia's expenses. This was something completely unexpected, and we were overwhelmingly grateful. Still, after two surgeries, our out-of-pocket bill was more than $12,000. That amount was shocking—and enormous—to us. We had no idea how we would pay such a bill, but we were committed to meeting our obligation.

When we first received the medical bills, I knew we could never pay the debt before Mia's next surgery when she would be about five years old. But we didn't waste any time and quickly set up a payment plan, diligently paying $100 per month. When Jase and I received Christmas bonuses or bonuses connected to one of our clients, or earned extra money working trade shows selling Duck Commander products, we put that money toward the medical bills. We were disciplined and dedicated to paying off that bill, and while it took years to pay it, we met our goal of paying off the first two surgeries right before her third one.

Starting School

Starting school is a big deal for any child, and Mia was no exception. The boys each attended St. Paul's Day School when they were four years old. Reed and I spent an entire day together visiting all of the church preschools in our area, and we both fell in love with St. Paul's. It was a very organized and scheduled environment, and the teachers there were almost dripping with sweetness. Within sixty seconds of walking in the door, I had made up my mind that this was where I wanted my children to start school. They went for a few hours three days a week, and it turned out to be the perfect place for Reed and Cole to begin their formal education.

When Mia was old enough, I was determined for her to have the same great environment that Reed and Cole experienced. Her first day at St. Paul's was a very big milestone for me. I have always taken a picture of each of my kids in their prospective classrooms or in the hallway on the first day of school every year (well, until they got into middle school and became absolutely horrified). This day was no exception. Mia looked absolutely adorable in a cute little skirt and shirt, and her smile that day told me that she was as excited for this day as I was.

Mia then joined her brothers at OCS the following year. She absolutely loved school and had definitely overcome her clinginess to me by that time. She had become a little social butterfly. Mia thoroughly enjoyed being with her friends, and she felt like a big girl, going to school like her brothers and older cousins. A highlight of her first year at OCS was when Mamaw Kay brought all the necessary ingredients for her famous homemade biscuits, and Mia and her class helped her make an entire batch. They all ended up covered in flour, especially Miss Kay!

Mia's biggest struggle when she started school involved how she formed the letters *f* and *v* when speaking. After Mia's initial work with her speech therapist as a baby, I paid close attention to the way she formed her words, determined to help her so her speech would not be a problem. As she grew older I started to notice that instead of making the *f* and *v* sounds by putting her top teeth to her lower lip, she made them by moving her lower teeth to her upper lip. The sounds seemed perfect, but I knew she was forming them improperly, so I worked to teach her to make them correctly.

When we saw Dr. Sperry later that year, she told me to stop correcting Mia because she was physically unable to make the sound as other people do. Because of the way her jaw was growing, she had an underbite, and making the sounds this way was normal for her. She had learned to compensate for her physical condition, something I did not realize right away.

I explained Mia's difficulty to her teacher and asked her not to correct her. The teacher gladly agreed. Mia still forms these sounds the same way she did when she started pre-K. Every year I ask her teachers not to correct her, and I appreciate that they are understanding and allow her to speak naturally.

A New Doctor, Another Surgery

During Mia's pre-K year at OCS, she was scheduled for her "touch-up," utilizing the new tissue that had grown around her lip area since her previous procedure and smoothing out the area cosmetically.

By that time, Dr. Salyer had retired, so we chose Dr. David Genecov, the son of Mia's orthodontist and a highly regarded surgeon for cleft lip and palate at ICI. Right away, we thought he was phenomenal in terms of both his surgical expertise and his bedside manner.

Mia did not remember her two previous surgeries at all. She did not know exactly what to expect, but she was aware of what was happening, and we talked about it openly. After we arrived at the hospital, they gave her goofy juice, which made her *really* goofy. She was funny, talking about animals coming to life and saying to Jase, "Daddy, you should meet them!"

Thanks to the goofy juice, Mia did not have a care in the world. When the time came for her to be taken back to the operating room, she simply said, "Bye, Mom!"

I was thankful for the chance to laugh with her, but I was also mindful of the heaviness of another surgery. Letting the medical staff take her back for the third surgery was as difficult emotionally for us as it had been for her first and second operations, but Jase and I hid it well from Mia until she was out of sight. Then, once again, we caved emotionally, especially knowing this would change her outer appearance once again. This time, however, we felt better prepared.

The surgery turned out to be more extensive than planned. We did not realize the possibility that Mia's nasal passages could still collapse after the palate had been repaired. But, to our surprise, they had. What we dodged during her second surgery came back to haunt us during her third. When it was over, Dr. Genecov had indeed touched up her lip area, but he also had inserted a hard stent into her nose. She ended up with more railroad track stitches, plus the stent sewn into her nasal passage.

This third surgery was more difficult on me than I expected it to be, mostly because I was not prepared for how she would handle the recovery.

I Should Have Prepared Her

Soon after we returned from Dallas, I stopped by Willie and Korie's house with Mia to pick up something. When I pulled in the driveway, Willie stuck his head through an open window to say hello to Mia. He is the one who came up with her nickname, Mia Moo, and often calls her by that name or "Moo Moo."

"Moo Moo, did you have your surgery?" Willie asked playfully.

My heart nearly broke when I turned and saw her try to hide her face from him. She has always loved Willie, so I knew she was ashamed of the way she looked. I tried to mask my tears as I pulled out of their driveway and into ours. That's one of the big differences between an infant who has surgery and a five-year-old or older child. The infant feels no shame. Once children are old enough to become self-conscious, they do struggle with the visible effects of an operation, and that becomes a whole new dynamic for both the patient and the family to deal with. This was something I was not prepared for.

After the incident with Willie, I realized we had entered a new phase of handling Mia's recoveries. After her previous operations, people had felt free to drop by with a meal or a gift for Mia or simply for a visit. That social interaction had been good for me. This time I said to Jase, "We don't need a lot of visitors right now. I have to figure out how to talk to her about this." Knowing that members of our church family were eagerly awaiting our arrival home so they could see Mia, bring her small gifts, and give us all encouragement, I called Alan and asked him to announce at the next church service that we were receiving no visitors for the next few days.

That same day, a couple of hours after our encounter with Willie, a wonderful godly woman named Joneal came to our door to drop off a present for Mia. I consider Joneal one of my mentors, so when I met her at the door and answered her greeting with silence and tear-filled eyes, she could see how hard the situation was. "You can do this, Missy," she said. "I know you. You're a strong woman. You can do this."

I simply nodded my head yes and closed the door.

Unlike the first surgery, I was prepared for what *I* would see after Mia's procedure. The problem was that Mia had no idea what *she* would see. The fact that she was not prepared for the way she would look hit me as hard as the first time I saw her after her surgery at three months. I remembered how shocked and upset I was at that time, so I could only imagine how she felt. I realized I should have done more to prepare her.

Now, whenever I have a chance to talk to parents whose children are scheduled for a surgery that will alter the way they look—even temporarily—I urge them to do their best to prepare their children ahead of time. That, for me, is one of the blessings of everything we have been through with Mia: I have the chance to help others avoid some of the mistakes I made, and that gives me a sense of purpose in the journey God has allowed Mia and our family to travel.

9

*A Recovery, a Reprieve,
and a Major Challenge*

WHEN I WITNESSED Mia's reaction to her swollen face with the protruding nose stent and stitches, I recognized that she needed to understand that this stage of her healing process was only temporary. Every chance I had, I encouraged her with comments such as "When your nose heals, we won't have to deal with that stent anymore" or "As soon as those stitches come out, you can go swimming again."

Mia wasn't old enough to have an in-depth conversation about how her current condition would ultimately improve her quality of life, so I had to put it into terms a five-year-old could grasp. Though the first couple of days at home were difficult, she adapted rather quickly and, surprisingly, wanted to play and find other activities to fill up the day. While I certainly had to take care of her after the previous operations, I didn't need to find ways to keep her occupied. This time was different. I definitely needed to keep her busy.

Although Mia wasn't happy about missing even one day of pre-K, I knew it was the best idea. I let her do whatever she wanted to do to pass the time—within reason. She received many gifts after her surgery, including a bracelet-making kit. The day we returned home from the hospital, she wanted the two of us to create bracelets for every female member of our family. Although I was exhausted from the trip, I couldn't refuse her request. So we sat at the dining room table for two solid hours of bracelet making. She put her best effort into each bracelet and meticulously wrote names on all of them with glitter paint. When we finished, she was so proud!

In addition to finding ways to help Mia spend her time at home, I had to deal with her newfound independence. Now she was able to express her opinion about things, and she was determined to do certain things herself.

When Mia was three and a half years old, we realized we had completely outgrown our home, and we purchased a larger, older house across the street from where Willie and Korie were building a new home. Jase and I agreed to take a leap of faith financially, knowing we would be in a more secure environment because we were close to family, especially when he was traveling for Duck Commander. The house had a pool, which the boys, now nine and twelve, enjoyed immensely. Reed and Cole were strong swimmers, but Mia hadn't learned how to swim, so we were concerned for her safety.

After listening to various people's advice about installing special gates and alarm systems, I finally decided the best defense was a good offense. So I taught Mia how to swim, beginning in the bathtub, showing her how to blow bubbles under the water each night. We "graduated" to the pool soon after and continued to work together.

Over the course of several weeks, she became a good swimmer for her age and gained confidence in the water. Even though she was young, the pool never intimidated her. She was determined to learn to swim, and she did. In fact, Mia was jumping off the diving board and swimming to the ladder before her fourth birthday, only three months after we had moved into the house with the pool. I guess it's safe to say that she gets a bit of her independence and determination from me.

There is a difference between independence and rebellion in a child, and Mia is not rebellious at all. She's quick to say, "I got this" and to take care of a situation to the best of her ability. I don't think her determination and independent spirit come from just one influence, but from many, including the many physical challenges she has faced. I also believe that her role as the third child in a busy family—whose dynamics were already in full swing by the time she came along—has much to do with how she handles herself. I'm convinced that she simply saw that the family train was already in full motion and decided that she had better find a way to hang on! All of these factors contribute to her character of independence, self-assuredness, determination, and boldness.

Mia's confidence blossomed in new ways as she recovered from her surgery. After we returned from the postoperative trip to Dallas to have her stitches and stent removed, she received a take-home stent that had to be cleaned every day—not a pleasant or easy process.

Mia wanted to clean her stent and care for her surgical wounds herself, with no help from me. In fact, she actually fought me on it, *begging* me to let her do it. I knew this was a good step for her, but it tried my patience because I could have completed the cleaning process much faster than she did.

The process involved removing the stent from her nose, washing it, and cleaning the blood and mucus from her nose with a cotton swab. Each day I sat and watched as she pulled off the tape that secured the stent, with her little hands shaking. She would start to do it, then talk herself out of it, then commit to doing it again, and then move forward. After she removed the stent, she hesitantly rolled the cotton swab in her nose to clean it. As a task-oriented person, I often thought, *Let's just get this done*, but Jase encouraged me to go easy on Mia and be patient with her, which I did as best I could. In the end, that was the right thing to do because it gave her a sense of control over her recovery.

"I Want to Go Back to School"

For a few days, Mia was happy enough at home, especially when she was making crafts or playing with her toys, but before long she started asking when she could go back to school. Her class had been so sweet to her while she was recovering, drawing pictures for her and trying to write her name on them. They did their best to support and encourage her in their five-year-old ways, and she missed them.

The problem with her going back to school so soon was that she had to wear her nasal stent every day for another month to keep her nasal passages from collapsing. I wasn't ready to expose her to what I thought would be finger-pointing and laughing and other children making fun of her. In addition, she wouldn't be allowed to do any physical activity because an injury at that point in her recovery could be a serious setback. All I wanted was to protect her.

After several days of Mia's pleas and my saying, "You can't go yet," I talked to her teacher and finally decided it was okay for her to return. That morning, she did not give a second thought to the very noticeable stent taped across her nose. It never bothered her—she was thrilled to be back in school.

In that situation I relearned an important lesson I first learned soon after she was born. Once again, I was trying to protect myself as much as I was trying to protect her. I wanted her to be spared the questions and potential ridicule of other children, while she wanted to get back into her routine and be with her friends. Only after I let her make the decision to return to school did I realize that that was exactly the right thing for her to do.

Once Mia recovered completely, she resumed her normal level of social activities. She not only continued to enjoy school and have fun with her friends, but she was also happily involved in our church activities. I describe her as "an active child who wants to be active." She loves life and wanted to be part of everything.

With two older brothers who were both athletic, Mia was familiar with sports. Since we spent many summer days and nights at the baseball fields, when Mia became old enough to join a softball league, she told us she really wanted to play. Jase began practicing with her in the yard, and after a few days, I asked him how she was doing.

"She'll get killed out there," he replied, thinking about tiny Mia playing with bigger, more aggressive kids. However, Jase did notice that she was a fast runner, so we introduced her to soccer, where she succeeded quickly and was on two consecutive championship teams. We were thankful that she had the opportunity to play those two years before her next big surgical procedure—a bone graft.

This Is Not Easy

When Mia was seven, Dr. Jeff decided to take the first steps for fitting her with braces and preparing her for "the biggie"—bone graft surgery. Mia's first orthodontist, Dr. Jeff's father, had retired by this time. She was now under the care of Dr. Jeff, who also happened to be our surgeon's brother. At our first appointment, he placed an expander in Mia's mouth. I was familiar with this common orthodontic apparatus. In fact, Cole had needed one, so I knew the routine of turning the key each night to increase the amount of space between the teeth.

A few months later, we returned to Dallas to see Dr. Jeff again. We learned that a fifteen-millimeter difference existed between the projection of Mia's upper jaw and her lower jaw, a major deficiency. Scar tissue had developed behind her upper jaw after the palatal surgery when she was seven months old and, as a result, had prevented her upper jaw from growing at the same rate as her lower jaw. In an effort to pull the upper jaw forward as much as possible before the bone graft surgery, Mia had to wear special headgear. This was not the usual type of orthodontic headgear many children wear at night; I can only describe it as "Hannibal Lecterish," a painful, harsh-looking piece of equipment that was difficult to imagine any human being having to wear.

The day Mia got her headgear, Dr. Jeff attached hooks to her teeth and showed us how to attach rubber bands in a way that would achieve the desired result. This, of course, made Mia's teeth very sore, and I could hardly stand the thought of her having to endure the pain of wearing it. She would have to wear the headgear twelve to fourteen hours a day for anywhere from a year to eighteen months. As long as her jaw was moving, she needed to wear it. When the movement hit a plateau, Dr. Jeff explained, we would know it was time for the bone graft surgery.

"Of course, Mia can take a break from the headgear once in a while," he said. "Say for one night if she has a friend over or for a special event." I knew this was going to be a problem because Mia often spent nights with her cousins, much more than "once in a while."

My mom was with Mia and me that day, and we left the

office for our regular four-and-a-half-hour drive home with Mia feeling uncomfortable because her mouth hurt and with me on the edge of tears, knowing what was in store for her for the next twelve months, if not longer.

As a precautionary safety measure, Mia would not be able to participate in any physical activity while she wore the headgear. No soccer, no riding her bicycle, no running and playing with her cousins, and no jumping on the trampoline with Bella, which was one of her favorite things to do. My heart was broken, knowing that the happy, carefree, fun lifestyle she enjoyed so much was going to change dramatically. I was relieved when Dr. Jeff told her she didn't have to wear the headgear to school, but she would have to put it on immediately when she got home from school, take it off only to eat dinner, and wear it through the night and up to the minute she left for school in the morning.

Early on in Mia's journey, I decided to enjoy the periods of time between surgeries without allowing myself to think about the next operation or to look too far ahead. I am thankful to say that I did that well, staying focused on all the good things about our family's life from day to day until those moments when I found myself sitting in a doctor's office hearing him say, "Here's what's next."

The headgear was a whole new set of circumstances. It was not a surgery, but it was not a worry-free time either. Every day we had a visual reminder of the procedure that lay ahead—and it was a big one. I knew I needed to accept this new dynamic of Mia's life, but I struggled greatly. Looking back, I know that Jase, Reed, and Cole were startled when they first saw Mia wearing it as well, but they kept their reactions hidden from her.

Not only was the headgear unattractive and intimidating looking, it was difficult to deal with. The rubber bands had to be attached in specific ways in order to pull her jaw forward correctly.

For more than a week after she got the headgear, I followed the routine vigorously with Mia when she came home from school. Every time I had to put it on her, she fought me. I hated having to do it because it caused her so much pain and always resulted in tears for both of us. I never let her see me get emotional, and I tried my best to keep my composure, but many times I had to turn away so I could wipe my own tears. She begged me to leave the headgear off for longer periods of time, but I knew I couldn't. Dr. Jeff had explained the importance of wearing it, and as a mom, I try to accept the facts as the doctors give them to me. I am committed to obeying doctors' orders.

I knew in my head that this grueling ordeal was the best thing for Mia, but my heart was a mess. I cried constantly. This was just not like me. *Get ahold of yourself,* I demanded in my head, followed the next moment by more tears and wondering, *What is wrong with me?* Jase and I prayed for strength and endurance, but I was having difficulty finding peace with the situation.

I have a strong circle of friends—my sisters in Christ—whom I can call on whenever I need them. Normally, I'm not one to ask for help, but at this time in my life I felt a desperation that demanded assistance. I sent a group message asking them to pray for me and lift me up to the Father. They immediately responded to me with words of encouragement and confidence that Mia and I could get through this. I knew they meant it, that they were going to follow through with their promise to pray for me. These women reached out, took my hand, and are still holding on to it today. They love me with all of their hearts, and I know how blessed I am to have them in my life.

Back to Dallas

A week after Mia received her headgear, we had to go back to Dallas for an annual checkup with Dr. Genecov. When he asked me how things were going with the headgear, I began to tear up, and I'm sure he could tell by my voice that I was having a difficult time.

Trying to be helpful, he said, "Well, our goal is to get her jaw to move a little more than one millimeter."

One millimeter? I was shocked and angry. "We are trying to get her jaw to move one millimeter—when it is fifteen millimeters deficient? This headgear has disrupted her entire life. And we are going through all this for *one millimeter?* What difference does one millimeter make?"

Possibly taken aback by my strong reaction, Dr. Genecov quietly replied, "Every millimeter counts."

I'm certain he could tell by my expression that his answer was not good enough for me.

He continued. "Any time we have to do the distraction surgery to correct more than ten to twelve millimeters, the chances of success are much lower. That is why every single millimeter counts." (During a distraction surgery, the patient's top jaw is broken and moved for better alignment with the lower jaw.)

While his explanation gave me a clearer picture of this situation, I still was not happy about this ultimate goal, and I thought the headgear was a lot to put Mia through for one millimeter. I immediately thought, *This is not acceptable to me. I am not ready to settle for one measly little millimeter!* My week of grieving was over. I was ready to get to work.

A Bold Request

Since the age of twenty, I have sung on the praise team at our church. Every Sunday morning before the worship service, the team prays together. If anyone has a particular need, the person can mention it, and the team will pray right then and there. The Sunday after Mia and I returned home from Dr. Genecov's office, I told the team about our situation. Then I made a bold request: "These expected results are not good enough for me. I need this headgear to break all records! I am asking y'all to pray this specific request—that Mia will not have to undergo the distraction surgery."

My fellow praise team members agreed to pray with me and faithfully prayed during the following weeks and months.

One point I emphasize when talking with moms of other children with special needs is that having a support system is not just important—it's crucial. The emotional aspects of having a child who must undergo surgery or treatments can be quite draining, and tending to a child's unusual physical needs can be exhausting. Feeling overwhelmed at times is to be expected—and it's okay.

The support system does not have to be large; it needs to be strong and dependable. I thank God for mine!

A Good Friend

One of Mia's favorite things to do is to spend the night with her cousins at Mamaw Kay's house. Not long after we returned from Dallas, I was picking up Mia and Bella from Jessica's house, where the two of them had spent the night. I had let Mia have the night off from wearing her headgear. As the girls were chatting in the backseat, I heard Bella tell Mia, "Mamaw Kay wants us to spend the night with her tonight, and she wants Lily and Merritt to come too."

Miss Kay goes all out when her granddaughters spend the night. For the girl cousins, Miss Kay's is *the* place to be. They absolutely love it because she really makes an effort so that their time together is special. She had turned the old Duck Commander offices into a "library" for them, housing hundreds of books, old cash registers, adding machines, and all kinds of abandoned equipment she used during the first years of running a business—the kind children love to play with. She also turned the old duck call and reed-making shop into the "Lickety-Split," a large playhouse in which each of her younger grandchildren has their own desk or play area filled with toys and projects. The name for this special place came about one day when the girls served me a plate of pretend food "prepared" in the playhouse. "Wow! That was lickety-split!" I said. Everyone agreed it was the perfect name. How many kids have two separate playhouses to encourage such creativity? Well, at Mamaw Kay's they do!

Mia was so excited at the thought of spending the night with all her cousins again. But when she asked me if she could go, I had to tell her no because she couldn't skip wearing her headgear two nights in a row. "You can spend the night with Bella, or Bella can spend the night with us, but I cannot let you go to Mamaw Kay's," I told her.

At that point, I was the only person who could help her get the headgear on and off. I could do that easily at Bella's house because she lives right across the street from us, but Phil and Kay live quite a distance away. "I can't send you to their house with that headgear unless you are ready to put it on and take it off by yourself."

Mia was crushed, and my heart broke for her. But I knew I could not allow her to be too far away from me quite yet.

Realizing Mia's disappointment, Bella piped up. "It's okay, Mia," she said. "I'll stay at your house tonight. I don't have to go to Mamaw Kay's." I knew instantly what a huge sacrifice that was for Bella, and I appreciated her thoughtfulness and kindness.

But Bella was not finished. "And I'll help you learn to take your headgear off and put it on," she continued.

"No, I can't do it," said Mia.

"Come on, Mia," said Bella, coaxing her cousin gently. "*We* can do it."

Quiet tears streamed down my face as I listened to this sweet interaction between these ten- and nine-year-old cousins. Bella was willing to give up a night in the Lickety-Split to help Mia learn how to manage this new phase in her life. If only adults could be this sacrificial!

Bella did spend the night with us and helped Mia learn to deal with her headgear. Mia mastered it within a couple of days. All she needed was a little encouragement and support, which Bella provided. This accomplishment gave Mia a new level of independence. She could now spend the night away from home whenever she wanted.

What I wasn't prepared for was Mia's next announcement: "I'm going to wear this to school."

Shocked and concerned about how other children would react when they saw her, I protested, "No, Mia. The doctor said that you don't have to."

But Mia had already thought the situation through. "Mom, if I wear it at school," she explained, "then I don't have to wear it when I get home from school, and I can play with Bella and ride my bike. I'll wear it during math and a couple more classes so I have more time to play when I get home. I mean, I'm just sitting at my desk anyway!"

I had to admit, even though I was nervous that people might make fun of her or ask inappropriate questions about her headgear, Mia's idea made sense. It was very practical, just like Mia. Once she got that plan in her mind, I could not talk her out of it.

Mia loves to be at school. She's extremely secure and self-confident; she really doesn't care what other people think about her. So we picked out a nice black-and-white bag and embroidered "Mia's Headgear" on it, and off she went to school to manage her headgear all by herself. She figured out exactly when to put it on and when to take it off in order to get in all of her required hours and still be able to take it off for lunch, recess, and physical education class. She had done the math and figured out that she would have three and a half hours to play, headgear-free, every afternoon after school.

It wouldn't be long before a situation arose that affirmed Mia and her decision.

"This Kid Is Phenomenal!"

One of Mia's classmates also needed to wear orthodontic headgear to correct an underbite. Although his headgear wasn't as complicated as Mia's, he didn't want to wear it as long as he needed to each day and balked at his mother's insistence.

A few days after Mia showed up at school in her headgear, the little boy's mother stopped me at school and told me how she had been struggling with her son about his headgear. "But last week he came home after school so excited and said, 'Mom, you will not believe what Mia has on!'"

"What?"

"Headgear! If she can do it, so can I!"

When I told Mia the story, her entire face lit up. She was so proud of herself, but more than that, she loves to help others. Knowing she had given someone else courage and strength was a great blessing to her.

During that year, we had an appointment with Dr. Sperry, whom Mia saw only once a year for speech evaluation. Before the visit I told Mia that the doctor would have lots of questions, and that she needed to be the one to answer them, not me.

Dr. Sperry did indeed have a lot of questions for Mia, which she answered in great detail—telling stories and being a bit sassy and funny. Every few minutes, Dr. Sperry would glance at me and grin.

Finally, she said to Mia, "Okay, are you ready to go see Dr. Genecov?"

"That's it?" Mia replied. She paused, then cut to the chase. "How'd I do?"

The doctor seemed confused by Mia's questions, so I explained.

"I told Mia she needed to answer your questions and speak freely because you were analyzing her speech."

Looking at Mia, Dr. Sperry said, "Let me tell you something, little girl. You have no need for speech therapy!"

"Sometimes, my teacher tells me to repeat something I said, but that's only when my headgear is on," Mia blurted out.

Dr. Sperry looked at me in disbelief. "She wears her headgear to school?"

I nodded.

"In my entire career here, I have never heard of a patient wearing headgear to school. In fact," she continued, "most children who come into my office keep their heads down and have a hard time looking me in the eye. The fact that Mia interacts with me in the way that she does *and* wears her headgear to school says a lot about her character. This kid is phenomenal!"

I knew she was a special kid. But I was learning more and more just how extraordinary she really was.

How Many Millimeters?

When Mia first got the headgear, Dr. Jeff sent us home with a form for us to record the exact hours Mia wore the headgear each day. At our first six-week checkup, I gave the sheet to the dental hygienist in Dr. Jeff's office before we went in to see him.

"Is this total correct?" she asked.

"Yes," I said. "Why do you ask?"

"Because no one ever wears it this much."

"But that's what you told us to do," I said.

"Yes, but no one *actually* does it. Most parents make their child wear it about 250 hours. Good job, Mom!" Mia's hours totaled 464.

What? Seriously? I was stunned. As much as I hated this headgear and how it was affecting Mia's normal lifestyle, I never gave a second thought to following the doctor's orders. I was astonished to learn that most parents don't, saying it's inconvenient or they don't want to fight with their child. I constantly try to see the big picture and understand why certain things must be done now in order to ensure good results in the long run. If an expert tells me something will benefit my child, I will do it. The headgear is an extremely challenging part of cleft lip and palate treatment, and I urge every parent who has to deal with it to do what must be done. It's not pleasant, but it is necessary, and it can save a child and a family a lot of additional trouble in the long run.

In fact, after that first checkup I decided to push Mia a bit more and told her that if she wore the headgear for 500 hours each six-week period, I would buy her an American Girl doll accessory when we went to Dr. Jeff for her checkup. That's all it took. She met the goal each and every time, and she has a basketful of American Girl doll clothes to prove it.

When Mia saw Dr. Genecov after a full year of wearing her headgear, he was amazed and so were we. Diligence, faithfulness, and lots of prayer from many people had worked a miracle. Mia's upper jaw—the one they wanted to move one millimeter—had moved a full *ten* millimeters! We broke the records.

10

The Biggie

FOR AS LONG AS MIA had been receiving medical care at ICI, we had heard about a procedure I refer to as the biggie—the bone graft surgery that would take bone from Mia's hip and graft it into her jaw. When Mia's jaw movement finally hit a plateau, we scheduled this major surgery for January 3, 2014.

Five years had passed since her lip touch-up, and during that time our lives had changed dramatically. Our family, once just a bunch of people trying our best to love God and love one another in our hometown of West Monroe, Louisiana, had become celebrities. That had changed our schedule and our financial situation, but for Jase and me, it had changed little else. We still held firm to our values and convictions, as we do to this day.

The Robertson family's early media exposure began about the time of Mia's five-year surgery. Duck Commander had been making hunting videos since 1988 and had a small but loyal following of fans, but our visibility increased when Benelli, a firearms company that makes shotguns and rifles, created a series called *Benelli Presents Duck Commander*. The program aired on the Outdoor Channel for three years and was the first of its kind to feature a reality aspect, which in this case included all of our family members.

When *Duck Dynasty* premiered on A&E in March 2012, our entire family found ourselves in the spotlight. It began with baby steps, but when the second season started, things began to snowball. By the first episode of season four—"Till Duck Do Us

Part," when Phil and Miss Kay renewed their marriage vows—12 million households were watching. For Jase and me, however, the celebrity status we enjoy has never been about fame and fortune. We are certainly glad our finances are not so tight anymore, and we do not have to worry about paying our medical bills as we did when Mia was a baby, but we were a happy family before our resources increased, and we will be happy when the current benefits of *Duck Dynasty* fade away. Our joy and security in life have never been tied to any material thing; they have always been in God and in our relationships with people, especially our family. We have not wanted to use our visibility to promote ourselves, but to point people toward God, to share our faith, and to raise awareness of cleft lip and palate. In our minds, those are the reasons God has allowed us the level of influence *Duck Dynasty* has provided.

No matter how much media exposure anyone has, it does absolutely nothing to make a difficult situation easier, especially when a child with medical needs is involved. Sure, we were on television, on one of the highest-rated shows on cable, but we still had to deal with Mia's condition. Being television personalities could not reduce the stress or anxiety of knowing our child had to face a major surgical procedure or make her challenges go away. When it came to Mia's surgery, Jase and I were just two ordinary parents concerned about our little girl.

But I realized there was one thing our celebrity status *could* do. If A&E would film the events surrounding Mia's bone graft surgery, we could help bring attention to the condition of cleft lip and palate. So we pitched the idea a few months prior to Mia's surgery. They balked.

"*Duck Dynasty* is a comedy show," they explained to us. "This situation with Mia's surgery isn't funny. We don't want to try to make it something people will laugh at."

They did have valid concerns, but I didn't agree with their decision. I felt that our audience could handle a more serious subject. I had met so many people who were interested in Mia that I was confident the episode would work. Besides, when we were doing shows with Benelli, they included an episode that featured both Mia's first surgery and Willie playing Santa Claus, comically struggling to get in his suit. It was a hit. The more we talked to A&E, the more everyone realized it might be a good idea. Mia's response? "Awesome!" The network arranged to send a single cameraman to capture the hospital segment on film for the longer episode. Normally, *Duck Dynasty* has four people behind the cameras, as well as numerous others who are handling lights, sound, and all other matters on the set. It seems like there are always about fifty people running around on the set. One cameraman would be perfect for the scene in the hospital.

But there was much more to that season-five finale, titled "Stand by Mia."

Standing by a Brave Little Girl

Jase and I asked Mia what she wanted to do before her surgery. "How about a family party?" she suggested. So the invitation went out. It's interesting when you mention to family members that they are going to be on TV—*schwoom*, they are there. As Willie said, "I didn't know we had this much family."

Mia had always heard the funny stories about Jase wrestling with his brothers and cousins growing up, particularly how cousin Amy beat up Willie, so that's what she requested for the special entertainment. As Jase said, "It's the ultimate redneck dinner theater." A wrestling ring was delivered, and the warm-up act was the Robertson boys clowning around, performing their best wrestling moves. Willie surprised everyone with guest professional wrestlers, including Jase's favorite, "Hacksaw" Jim Duggan.

I felt kind of bad for them, wearing only their little wrestling pants, while the rest of us were bundled up in winter coats. Yes, it was January, but it was unusually cold in Louisiana—about twenty degrees. The wrestlers had to keep moving fast; otherwise, they would have frozen to death!

At the end of the party, Mia took the stage between Jase and Willie, thanking everyone for coming and then sharing from her heart: "My favorite verse is Psalm 46:10: 'Be still, and know that I am God!' God is bigger than all of us, and He is bigger than any of your struggles, too." I think I can say that there was hardly a dry eye in the crowd. Going into her surgery, Mia was being brave for all of us. In the end, seeing the final version of the episode, I thought the network did a great job of including enough humor to make people laugh but also providing a tender glimpse into the love our family shares with one another and the love we all have for Mia.

When *Duck Dynasty* fans saw it on March 26, 2014, they agreed completely!

∞

A few days before we left home, Mia asked me, "Do I really have to have this surgery?"

I could tell she truly wanted to know whether it was absolutely necessary, so I stopped what I was doing and looked her straight in the eye. "As much as you don't want to have it, and as much as I don't want you to have to have it either, you have to do this for the quality of your life to be the best it can possibly be—for the rest of your life."

Expecting a long serious conversation about this, I waited for Mia's response.

"Okay," she said and darted out of the house to play.

She did not need a long conversation; she simply needed to know the truth.

Better than I Thought

During one of our preoperative visits with Dr. Genecov, I asked him, "Remember that new procedure you mentioned to us once, the one you were working on to make the bone graft procedure easier and less painful for patients? Did you ever perfect that?"

"Oh yes," he said, "I've been doing that procedure for quite some time." I didn't realize that this was his plan for Mia, too.

The doctor would take the bone from a different part of the hip than traditionally used, resulting in less discomfort and quicker healing for Mia. What a welcome piece of news!

"Will she still have to go to physical therapy?" I asked.

"No. Those days are over," he said. "She will have a pain pump, like a little ball, hooked to her hip for the first three days after surgery that will dispense medication regularly. After that, Mia will still have some pain, but she should get over it quickly and be able to get up and walk around."

I knew about the pain ball, and I was all for it! Cole had undergone shoulder surgery six months earlier, and he had used a pain ball for three days. It worked well for him, and I was glad to know Mia would have the same pain management.

Letting Her Go Again

On the day of Mia's surgery, the waiting room was filled with people, mostly our family and friends. This surgery took place in a new building, where the waiting area was family friendly, comfortable, and spacious enough for lots of guests.

The hospital staff allowed our cameraman, whom we affectionately call Burnsey, and our entire family to visit Mia in the preoperative holding area. We had all grown to love Burnsey on the set of *Duck Dynasty*, and Mia felt completely at ease having him there filming the moment. She was happy and relaxed, posing for photos for us to tweet, and seemed glad to have more company than usual prior to an operation. The dose of goofy juice started working fairly quickly, and everyone filed out of the room so Jase and I could have a moment alone with her. She made some hilarious comments that kept Jase and me laughing.

One of the effects of the goofy juice was slurred speech, and after numerous attempts of trying to figure out exactly what she was trying to say, we gave up. When Dr. Genecov came in to prep us on the surgery, our focus turned to him. Suddenly, realizing we were ignoring her, Mia hollered out in her drunken-like state, "I have a demand!"

"What do you need?" I said.

"I need to brush my teeth." That said, she conked out for a few minutes more.

As I've mentioned, the hardest moment for me during any surgery is saying good-bye to Mia before they take her back to the operating room. I had been through it a few times now, but never with such a big crowd and never on camera. The day of the biggie, Mia was groggy but still awake. Surrounded by Burnsey and all of our family, Jase and I both leaned down, kissed her, and said good-bye. As they started to wheel her away, Mia suddenly asked, "Am I going back now?"

I panicked, startled by her unexpected moment of clarity. I did not know how long she would be awake or how she might handle being alone in an unfamiliar place with a lot of strangers around her. Trying to be reassuring, I said as calmly as possible, "Yes, you are. I love you!"

"I love you, too," Mia said to Jase and me.

This was the first time any of our family members had been able to watch this process up close. Most of them with tears in their eyes, they all started telling her, "Bye, Mia." "We love you, Mia." "You're going to do great." It was one of the sweetest moments in my memory but also one of the most emotional. Quietly, we all headed to the waiting area.

Within a few minutes, a member of the medical staff came from the operating room and told me Mia was fine and didn't express any fear before she went to sleep. That, of course, was very comforting to hear.

During the operation, we were surrounded with activity and support. Some people simply sat with us, relaxing and talking, while others offered to get us something to eat or attend to any other needs we had. Miss Kay sat on the floor playing games with Mia's cousins. A few fans and a couple of nurses recognized our family and stopped to say hello and give us an encouraging word.

For some reason, this procedure seemed to go much more quickly than Mia's other surgeries. Maybe this was because all of our family and friends were doing a great job at keeping us occupied, or maybe it was because I had expected the biggie to be a more drawn-out procedure. Whatever the reason, I was thankful.

When Dr. Genecov came out and told us the surgery had

been "textbook, no complications at all, nothing unexpected," we were relieved and grateful. We all joined hands, and Alan led us in a prayer of thanksgiving to our almighty Creator.

I assumed Mia's face would be swollen, as it had been after previous operations, so I prepared myself. Because of what we expected to see, we had asked Burnsey not to film Mia after the procedure.

Before Jase and I were allowed into the recovery room, Burnsey came up to me and said, "Missy, I just saw her. She looks amazing!"

Wait! How did Burnsey see Mia before Jase and I did? It turns out that he had left some of his paperwork in one of the rooms not far from the recovery area. When he went to get it, he just happened to catch a glimpse of her. I knew Burnsey's excitement for Mia's well-being was completely genuine—he loved our family and especially Mia.

Custom-Made for Mia

One of my best friends is LinDee Loveland, who is a Bible teacher at OCS and the children's minister at our church. She and another friend and teacher, Mrs. Rita, were there at the hospital with us. As soon as they heard that everything had gone well, the two of them gathered all of Mia's cousins together.

"Missy, what's Mia's room number?" LinDee asked.

I rattled it off, then quickly caught up with Jase, who was heading to the recovery room.

We spent an hour in the recovery room with Mia, and when she was ready to be moved to her regular hospital room, Jase and I walked beside her gurney. When we walked into her room, I burst into tears. Mia's room was beautiful!

Several weeks before Mia's scheduled surgery, Mrs. LinDee had asked the children at church to make snowflakes that would be given to a child who needed some encouragement. Mia even made one herself and signed it. "Each individual snowflake is special, and no two are alike," Mrs. LinDee told them. "It's the same way with us," she shared. "No two people are alike. God makes everyone unique and special, with a purpose designed to glorify Him."

Later, when Mia wasn't there, she asked all the children to make cards for Mia. When LinDee and the cousins scooted out of the waiting room, they went straight to Mia's room and hung up the cards and the snowflakes all over her room. Mia was awake by the time she got back to her room, and when she saw the decorations, she literally oohed and ahhed.

Dr. Sperry and Dr. Genecov both made the same comment when they visited Mia later. "I've never seen a room like this! This is the most decorated room that's ever been in this hospital!"

And Dr. Sperry summed it up beautifully: "Wow, somebody must really love you."

Having a room decorated means so much to a child—and maybe even more to a child's parents. The fact that so many of Mia's friends had created such exquisite, handmade snowflakes and worked so hard to make cards for her, and that Mrs. LinDee, Mrs. Rita, and all the cousins surprised us with the final display, spoke volumes to me about the way people loved Mia and our family. That expression of creativity was not only beautiful, it also touched my heart deeply.

Post-Op Realities

For the next several hours, family and friends stopped by Mia's room to wish her well and check on us before they headed home. Everyone told her they loved her and were proud of her, and they kissed her on their way out the door. Once they had gone, only Jase and I, Reed and Cole, my parents, and Bonny were left, and we were tired but thankful after a long day.

That afternoon I noticed swelling on the right side of Mia's face, where her complete cleft is. Swelling in that area was not unusual after surgery, but it was still hard to look at. The swelling continued from Friday to Monday, to the point that Mia could not even open her right eye. She looked like someone had punched her! At one point Mia looked at me and moaned, "My life is miserable."

That was a tough statement to hear from my child, and my heart ached for her. As much as I wished with all my might that I could snap my fingers and instantly heal her, I couldn't. However, she needed some hope from me.

Holding back my own tears, I said, "I know you feel miserable right now, but you are going to get past this part. And when you do, your life is going to be much better than you ever could have expected it to be."

I knew that her hip wasn't bothering her very much because of the pain ball, but her mouth was beginning to hurt as the anesthesia wore off and the swelling began. On top of those things—and this is a big deal for Mia—she knew she could not have anything she wanted to eat. Being hungry and thirsty probably contributed as much to her misery as the effects of the surgery.

Mia's favorite drink is Dr. Pepper. As soon as the nurse told us she could have something other than clear liquids, we had a Dr. Pepper ready for her. She took two sips, grimaced through her pain, then said, "This tastes horrible!" For two days, she wouldn't even touch it.

The hospital stay was difficult but bearable. It was hard for

Mia because of her discomfort and because nothing tasted good to her. It was hard for the rest of us because we could tell how unhappy she was, how much pain she was in, and how much she was struggling. However, by the next day, she had made known to everyone that she was ready to go home.

Mia Puts Her Foot Down

As we were getting Mia's things ready for her discharge, her nurse started to excuse herself to get a wheelchair to transport Mia to the car. Instantly, Mia said, "I'm not riding in a wheelchair."

"Yes, you are, Mia. It's a hospital regulation," I said, believing that was true.

"Mom," she protested, "they said I'm supposed to walk as much as possible. I'm walking to the car."

I saw a certain look in Mia's eyes as she made this announcement, the look that says "I am going to push hard for this." I knew she was determined, and I would fight a losing battle to try to talk her out of it.

"I'm walking out of here," she said again.

I guess the medical staff noticed that look too because they allowed her to try to walk, with a nurse close beside her. Seeing that little girl limp her way down the hall, holding Reed's hand, was one of the proudest moments of my life. I was absolutely amazed by her spunk and determination. I grabbed my cell phone from my purse and snapped a picture.

She is such a fighter, I thought as Jase and I followed her. Visually, she looked roughed up, as though she had been through about fifteen rounds in a boxing match. But in that moment, she showed a level of toughness and resilience I have never seen in a child.

Remembering the information we were told on that first visit to ICI when Mia was seventeen days old, that she would need physical therapy to help her walk again after this surgery, I thanked God as I watched our daughter walk right out of the hospital twenty-four hours postoperation!

When we got into the car, Jase asked Mia, "Well, what do you think about that?"

"I'm a little tired, but I made it," she replied. Indeed she did.

Continued Recovery

Once we returned home, I did not think Mia would be back to her old self for a couple of weeks, but she bounced back more quickly than I expected. Her surgery was on Friday, she was released on Saturday, and by the following Monday she started asking when she could go back to school. I knew that was a good sign, but I also knew she was nowhere near ready. After all, we were in the middle of winter (flu season), and she had just come off of a pain ball. *It's going to be a while*, I thought.

The Wednesday of that week was no different from other Wednesdays in our household. Each week since Reed's freshman year in high school, Jase and I had cooked dinner for a few of his fellow football teammates after practice. At first the group included just a few guys, but within a couple of years it grew to include cheerleaders and other friends as well. We fed them well and then took them all to church with us. It had become a regular event that we all enjoyed.

The Wednesday after Mia's surgery, she asked, "Are the teenagers coming tonight?"

"Yes," I told her. By that time, Jase and I had been through ten years of Mia's condition and surgeries. We were committed to doing everything we could do for her, but also for the boys, even when Mia was in recovery, because we wanted them to know that the things that were important to them were important to us, too. We knew they had to make certain sacrifices and adjustments because of Mia's needs, but we were determined from the beginning to minimize them and not to allow one special-needs child to wield excessive or undue influence over the other members of the family. So even though we were less than a week out from Mia's surgery, we weren't going to disrupt our regular dinner with Reed's friends.

"I'd better go get ready!" Mia exclaimed, heading upstairs to her room. When she returned, she was wearing the dress she had received for Christmas, and she had done her hair. Her face was still swollen, but it was becoming less noticeable.

By the end of that week, Mia was begging to go back to school. Ten days after her surgery, I allowed her to go two half days to see how she did with her eating. She proved to me that she could handle it, so the next week she started back full-time.

Mia knew that when she went back to school she would not be able to participate in recess or PE. "That's fine," she said. "I'll just read."

The limitations on Mia's physical activity at school applied at home, too. She could not run, ride a bicycle, or jump on the trampoline with Bella. She also had to skip gymnastics class each week, but she was able to continue her piano lessons. As a budding musician, this was very important to her.

Generally speaking, Mia's attitude throughout her recovery was phenomenal, but she was especially sad about the restriction with the trampoline. Once again, Bella came through in an amazing gesture of solidarity. She offered to stop jumping on the trampoline until Mia was given the go-ahead from the doctor. The trampoline is visible from our house, so anytime Bella jumps on it, Mia can see her and usually runs over to join her. Bella assured Mia that they would find something else fun to do. Her cousin's show of support meant a lot to Mia and made that aspect of her recovery much easier.

One activity the two of them enjoyed was playing with some of the gifts Mia received from people all over the country. Jase and I couldn't believe everyone's generosity and caring concern for our child. Like other people in the entertainment industry, we hear a lot from our fans. For someone to take time to send a gift or a card to Mia—well, we viewed each of those people as way more than a fan. This was not about people who simply enjoyed our television show; it revealed to us that our family had become meaningful to countless other families—and that was very special to us.

Three months is a long time for anyone to recover from surgery. You might think the biggest challenge of this recovery was keeping an active child from participating in all of her normal activities. That would be wrong. The biggest challenge of her recovery was an altogether different kind of battle, one that I was not sure we were going to conquer.

II
The Road to Recovery

WHEN I FIRST FOUND OUT the scheduled date for Mia's big surgery, I felt the pressure of one particular aspect of her recovery—her eating. Even though Mia bounced back well emotionally and had no complications with her physical healing process, trying to feed her was not just a daily challenge; it was a meal-by-meal, snack-by-snack ordeal.

By this point on Mia's journey, I had met numerous parents whose children had already undergone the bone graft surgery, some having the traditional procedure and others the less invasive method Dr. Genecov was now using. I had heard plenty of stories of how painful the procedure was and how long and difficult the recovery would be.

During our preoperative visit, we had met with a nutritionist who explained what Mia's ideal post-op diet should be. I already knew Mia would need to be on a liquid diet for three months, and the nutritionist gave us a goal of a minimum of 1,500 calories per day. Because the body burns more calories than usual when it is going through a healing process, it was critical for Mia to get this amount of nutrition each day.

Although she was ten years old, Mia's size was comparable to that of a seven-year-old. I knew that keeping her weight up wouldn't be easy, especially since she has always been a picky eater. Finding nutritional liquids that she would actually be willing to consume would prove to be a challenge, as she liked only three liquids: Dr. Pepper, apple juice, and water—none of which would provide the nourishment she needed. I had talked with Mia's pediatrician and with our team at ICI, and they assured me that the weight issue was something we had to take seriously. We truly could not allow her to lose even a few pounds.

Children with cleft palates are born with misaligned teeth. Mia's teeth are positioned all over the roof of her mouth, clumped together on one side, with the other side almost completely vacant. It's a long process to get the teeth where they need to be. As you can imagine, this makes eating extremely difficult for her. She doesn't bite her food like most people do. She tears it or breaks it with her fingers and puts small pieces into her mouth. She has done this for years, and we've gotten used to the fact that it takes her much longer to finish a meal than everyone else.

I'm not sure why Mia has such a limited diet. She refuses to try anything new, including most sweets, and is very particular about certain foods. For example, she will eat processed fish sticks, but she will not eat fresh fish that Jase catches. This really upsets Jase, especially since he comes from a family who lives to eat! Even Reed and Cole throw up their hands in frustration because they think she is just being stubborn.

The list of food Mia will eat is very short: chicken strips or nuggets, macaroni and cheese, cheese pizza, a few varieties of Chef Boyardee, and a few things I make at home, such as spaghetti and taco salad. That's pretty much it. Knowing what I go through normally to feed her, I was extremely anxious about her upcoming restrictive diet. I anticipated a battle.

When we were meeting with the nutritionist, she had suggested Mia drink Ensure or Boost or a similar nutritional supplement. Mia's eyes widened, and she began to shake her head fast at me in a silent but emphatic no, while I thought, *Yes, we need to do this.* I finally told Mia that if she refused to eat, she would end up back in the hospital—with a feeding tube. That was not a threat; it was a fact. She knew how high the stakes were.

Not only did Mia have to be on a liquid diet, she had to do it without letting anything touch or pass her upper lip. She could not use a straw or purse her lips on a spoon; she had to pour liquid into her mouth from a cup that rested on her bottom lip. That was difficult on its own! I could not blame her for not being enthusiastic about this recovery.

I've Got an Idea!

I had to get creative and expand her culinary choices. A couple of weeks before Mia's surgery, I invited a few of her friends and cousins over for a "soup-tasting sleepover" to generate peer support for her. I decided to focus on soups because they are fairly easy to make and can be loaded with healthy ingredients. Of course, Mia had hardly ever eaten soup in her life, but I wasn't going to let that stop the experiment. I was hopeful that some of the girls would enjoy the different varieties and say, "Wow! This is great!" so Mia would at least be willing to try them.

I spent all afternoon making four homemade soups, took extra time setting the table, and did every little thing I could think of to make it fun for everyone. This wasn't merely a meal; it was an event. I admit I was hoping that the girls being there would work in our favor. All of them were really excited about this—except Mia. She did *not* think it was fun at all.

The girls sat around our kitchen table in their cute pajamas, ready for the taste test to begin. I didn't identify any of the soups but asked them to figure out what kind it was and then to rate each variety on a scale of one to four, with one being not very good at all and four being a soup they really liked. I gave them a bowl of cheese soup because Mia really likes queso, and cheese is one of the foods she will eat happily. I also made tomato basil soup from scratch, a spaghetti sauce soup based on Miss Kay's homemade recipe, and a loaded baked potato soup, whipped and thinned as much as possible.

All of the girls loved rating the soups, except for Mia. All I wanted from her was a thumbs-up or a thumbs-down. She gave the cheese soup a wavering thumbs-up and the tomato basil a definitive thumbs-down. She did not like the potato soup at all. Actually, none of them did. (I guess mashed-up, liquefied potatoes aren't appealing to anyone!) I expected her to like the spaghetti sauce soup because my spaghetti is one of her very favorite meals. She did like it, especially because I smothered the top with grated, melted cheese.

Mia's friends liked three of the four selections. Mia only liked two of the four, but I was thrilled. *Good,* I thought, *I have two soups I can feed her for the next three months.* Her menu was not going to have much variety, but I was used to that. I just wanted her to eat. With two soups that I could alternate, a plain homemade vanilla milkshake, and some Ensure she reluctantly agreed to drink each day, I thought we were off to a good start. We struggled all the way through that three-month period, but we made it. Not only was Mia able to maintain her weight, she actually gained weight! When Dr. Sperry found out about this, she mentioned again that Mia had accomplished another "first" in her career. While I was completely thrilled about Mia's accomplishment, my joy was short-lived.

An Even Bigger Surgery

Two weeks after Mia's big surgery, we returned to Dallas for a checkup with Dr. Genecov. He was pleased with how everything looked. "After she recovers fully," he said, "we will start the process of the distraction surgery, which will take place within a year."

That was not what I wanted to hear. I had hoped the ten millimeters of movement of Mia's upper jaw might make the next procedure unnecessary. Dr. Genecov explained, "Her jaw is still eight millimeters deficient. It's only five millimeters deficient from top to bottom, but a perfectly normal alignment is a three-millimeter overbite."

"Instead of another surgery, could we try the headgear again?" I asked, hoping there might be another possible solution.

"Since Mia has had the bone graft surgery already, I don't think it would be effective at all," he replied honestly.

To help put my worry in perspective, I need to share an encounter I had with another mother the day before Mia's bone graft surgery. Mia was undergoing her pre-op appointment with the hygienist before she and I met with Dr. Jeff. While my parents and I were waiting for Mia to finish, a mother approached me, saying she recognized me from *Duck Dynasty.* She went on to say that her son had just undergone the distraction surgery.

"We've been told that Mia will most likely have that surgery in about a year," I sympathized. "How is your son doing?"

Hesitantly, she asked if I would like to see a picture of him. "Of course," I replied.

She showed me a picture of a boy, not too much older than

Mia, with a metal device called a halo that encircled his head with an additional piece that went into his mouth.

It resembled Mia's headgear, but this device looked much more uncomfortable to me.

"Does it come off at night?" I asked.

"No," the mom said. "It is screwed into his skull."

I instantly grew sick to my stomach. *How in the world will Mia be able to deal with this?*

When I asked the mom how her son was doing, she teared up. "Not too well. He is depressed. He won't eat, and he refuses to go to school."

As much as I wanted to comfort this struggling parent, I couldn't. Thoughts rushed through my mind. *I can't deal with this right now. I cannot handle this. I have to concentrate on Mia and the biggie that's staring us right in the face!* Just when I was about to lose it, Dr. Jeff came to the door and called me to come back. I didn't know how we were going to get through that future surgery. All I could permit myself to think about right then was the bone graft. However, the image of that boy became embedded in my mind, like it had been seared there with a red-hot branding iron. I *did not* want Mia to have to undergo that surgery, so I started praying fervently—again—for God to deliver us.

I decided right then not to tell Mia about the distraction surgery. Once her stent was removed after her three-month recovery, her orthodontist began placing braces on her teeth, just a couple at a time. We resumed our regular appointments with Dr. Jeff, and even though we still had to attend these visits, Mia was completely healed from her bone graft and was back to her everyday, normal activities. It was like a honeymoon period, an escape from thinking about the inevitable, and I was determined we were going to enjoy it. But no matter how hard I tried, I could not forget the unavoidable next step around the corner.

Good News and Bad News

A few weeks after the bone graft surgery, still recalling that picture of the little boy, I asked Dr. Jeff how certain he was that Mia would need the distraction surgery.

"Is this something she can live without?" I pleaded.

"This surgery needs to be done," he answered sympathetically. "It will benefit her greatly, not only in terms of correcting her speech, but her profile will look completely different."

Seeing the emotion in my eyes as I listened to his words, he added, "You are praying people. I've seen the results. If anybody can change this, it's you guys."

He was right. Our specific prayers had been answered before. Why wouldn't they be answered this time? Again, I enlisted my support circle to join me in praying that Mia's jaw would grow sufficiently so that she would not have to have this surgery. Confidently, we started praying.

For the next eight months, Mia and I made the long drive to Dallas for appointments with Dr. Jeff every six weeks. The time and distance of these trips never bothered me. What *was* difficult for me was that almost every checkup involved some type of adjustment or procedure that was hard for Mia, such as pulling a tooth or adding a brace. Whenever I would start getting emotional, I had to remind myself that each of these measures, whether big or little, was one more step toward the best possible quality of life for my daughter. In an effort to make each trip more pleasant for Mia, I'd invite either one of her cousins or a friend to come with us, and we would usually include a stop at the American Girl store in Dallas.

∞

On December 16, 2014, almost eleven years to the day that Mia had her very first surgery to correct her lip, we drove to Dallas for our annual checkup with Dr. Genecov. My mom was with us, and we met Bonny and her daughter, Tori, at our hotel the night before our appointment.

We turned in early after dinner. I didn't sleep well at all, but I did pray a lot. I could tell simply by looking at Mia that her jaw had not grown the desired amount. She wasn't aware of the distraction surgery because I couldn't bear to tell her about it. It was practically impossible for me to form the words when talking to someone else about it. I knew I had to be strong for my daughter, but every time I even thought about discussing it with her, I would start crying. I decided that whatever Dr. Genecov told us, Mia and I would hear and deal with it together.

That night, I lay in bed praying, pleading with God to help me get through the appointment the next day with strength and courage. *Lord, help me find the strength to hold it together for the sake of my daughter. Help me deal with what I am going to hear tomorrow so I can be the rock that my child needs. Help me . . .*

The next morning, while everyone else sat in the waiting area, Mia and I met with the doctor.

"Well, I have good news and bad news," Dr. Genecov said. "The bad news is that she needs this surgery, and we need to get it on the books right now. The good news is that I've worked with a company to invent a new device. Instead of using the halo, I can now do everything internally."

What? Did I just hear what I think I heard?

He continued talking, but I honestly didn't hear anything for the next few seconds while I tried to process this new information.

Seriously? I can't believe this! I thought. *Where did this come from? I knew he was working on a better bone graft procedure before we needed it, but this just came out of nowhere!* I tried my best to hold myself together. All I wanted to do was call Jase and tell him this news. Actually, I wanted to climb the nearest mountain (if there were mountains in Dallas) and shout it from the top of my lungs!

After thanking him profusely, Mia and I walked down the hall for our appointment with Dr. Sperry.

"Do you know what you just avoided?" Dr. Sperry asked, grinning from ear to ear. "A shaved head, the intensive care unit for a week, and a much longer recovery period."

That was it. I couldn't hold back any longer and let my tears flow. Mia looked at me in surprise. If I was embarrassing her, I didn't care. It was for a good reason.

"Dr. Genecov has been working hard to perfect this procedure, and he has done it one time so far." She looked right at Mia and said, "And I'm convinced he did that one to get ready for you."

Mia smiled and said, "Cool."

Mia had enjoyed her honeymoon period. She felt no stress or anxiety about the future, which was a great blessing. I was thankful that I had not told her about the distraction surgery and glad that my eleven-year-old daughter didn't understand all that she had been spared because of this development.

When I filled in my mom, Bonny, and Tori on this unexpected and exhilarating news, they all gasped, then shouted and hugged me.

All I could think of was how grateful I was to my Father in heaven. He had done this. Why? I don't know. But I knew He had chosen this moment for Dr. Genecov to perfect a new invention that would spare my daughter, at this exact time in *her* life, the ordeal of a device that would have been surgically screwed into her skull.

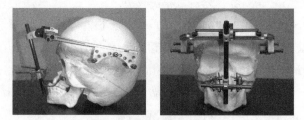

The rigid external distraction device commonly called a halo.

After getting to the parking lot, I immediately called Jase with this incredible news. Like me, he was having a hard time wrapping his head around it.

"How many of these has he done?"

I hesitated, then said, "One."

"One? He's done *one*? I don't know about this, Missy."

I quickly reminded him of Dr. Genecov's success in the new bone graft surgery and said, "Babe, I think it's worth the risk. He's proven to us just how good he is."

Jase is not one to make a quick decision about anything, but before our phone call ended, he agreed that we should move forward with the surgery.

Never a Good Time

Dr. Genecov wanted to schedule Mia as soon as possible, but we convinced him to let her finish her competitive cheer season first. Mia had excelled rapidly in her gymnastic skills and was proud for her team that had advanced to two national competitions. We decided that we could push out the surgery date so she could compete in the first competition but not the second. Her team and coaches understood and were very sweet and supportive, giving Mia a framed picture of the team inscribed with encouraging words. We scheduled the surgery for March 27, 2015.

As you can imagine, our family calendar fills up quickly and extensively. We not only have our immediate family responsibilities, like ballgames, school duties, and church activities, but there are also professional responsibilities that include filming, as well as speaking engagements and national media appearances. Around the time of Mia's surgery, these events included the Duck Commander 500 NASCAR Sprint Cup race in Fort Worth, Texas, as well as opening night of the *Duck Commander Musical* in Las Vegas, all of which would have to be put on the back burner. Jase and I would just have to figure out how to juggle it all while keeping Mia's health and well-being our top priority.

For me, the biggest conflict with the surgery date was that it fell on the same day as Cole's junior/senior formal at school. The formal had been a big night for Reed two years earlier, with the highlight being a special ring ceremony. Juniors receive their senior rings and ask two special people in their lives to turn the ring on their finger. Reed had asked me to be one of those two people for him, which was a special honor for me. *If Cole wants me there, I will reschedule Mia's surgery.*

"Cole, who are you planning on having turn your ring?" I asked.

"I didn't get a ring, Mom. I really don't want one," Cole replied.

Seriously? I thought. *Boy, are you your father's son or what?*

"All I really care about is getting some really good pictures."

I knew Cole was telling me the truth. He is not about fanfare or rituals. But he did want to remember the night.

"Absolutely! I'll make sure we have plenty of pictures of you," I exclaimed.

As it turned out, I think he was the most photographed student that night. Since I could not be there in person, people texted, e-mailed, and tagged me on Facebook with pictures of him. Again, my friends and Cole's friends' parents did what they could to help us through this difficult time. Something as simple as taking pictures was priceless to me. Yes, Cole was completely fine with my not being at the formal, but he was also sad that he could not be at the hospital for Mia. I assured him that there's never a good time for surgery, and he shouldn't feel guilty about attending his event—all of us wanted him to go and have a great time.

Mia's Confidence and Courage

On March 26, 2015, Jase, my parents, and I got Mia ready and headed to Dallas for a day of preoperative appointments. After listening to the details of the upcoming procedure and recovery, Jase and I quickly realized that, while enjoying a sense of euphoria after learning about the elimination of the halo, we had underestimated the seriousness of this procedure. During the two-and-a-half-hour procedure, Dr. Genecov would break Mia's upper jaw into three pieces, move it forward about three millimeters, then secure it with this new device. After spending the first twenty-four hours in intensive care, Mia would be moved to a regular room for the next night and, if all went well, could go home the following day.

After a full day of information and filling prescriptions with much of our extended family in tow, we asked Mia where she wanted to have dinner. She chose the Capital Grille, a place that our extended family thought was perfect. I mean, who doesn't love lobster mac and cheese?

Our sizable group was scattered among three different tables, and because the restaurant was a bit noisy, the kids' table didn't hear Alan lead us in the blessing. So Miss Kay went over to their table and led Mia and her cousins in their own prayer, thanking God for the food and asking Him to watch over Mia the next morning. After she finished, she asked the girls if they wanted to add anything. Mia said that she did. They all bowed their heads while Mia prayed for Mrs. Cathy, a dear friend of ours who was recovering from a recent mastectomy and undergoing chemotherapy for stage two breast cancer.

Miss Kay came over to me and Jase with tears in her eyes, recounting what Mia had prayed. "I just assumed she was going to pray for herself, but she prayed for Cathy instead."

When I told Miss Kay that we pray for Cathy each night at bedtime, Kay said, "Well, I guess Mia thought there was no reason that this night should be any different."

She also mentioned that she asked Mia if she was nervous about the next day.

"Not really" was Mia's response.

"But what *do* you feel?" Miss Kay asked her.

"Nothing. I just don't feel anything, really."

I guess I would interpret her response simply as Mia being at peace.

∞

Jase, Mia, and I arrived at the hospital early the next morning to what seemed like a replay of Mia's surgery one year earlier—same hospital, same preoperative area, and same room setup. Over the next few minutes, her room filled up with people, including Reed and his girlfriend of three and a half years, Brighton, who had both driven in from college. Mia loves being silly with them, and I snapped a picture of the three of them. Mia's cousins also surrounded her to play a game of Old Maid, thanks to the deck Mamaw Kay pulled out of her purse. Everyone was cracking jokes, taking pictures, and, well, just being themselves. All this activity helped keep Mia, as well as me and Jase, thinking positively and staying upbeat.

Mia opted to not take the goofy juice this time. She told me she wanted to be awake and alert so she could tell everyone good-bye as she was being rolled back through the operating doors. Whoa! I wasn't so sure about this. Jase thought it was very brave of her and that we should let her do it. Reluctantly, I agreed.

Dr. Sykes, the anesthesiologist, said he would tell her every single thing he was going to do before he gave her enough gas to first make her silly and then to put her to sleep. She was all for it.

However, as Dr. Sykes rolled her away, tears formed in Mia's eyes. I had to keep myself from shouting my thoughts: *Wait! Are you sure about this, Mia? You don't have to go in like this! Let's rethink this goofy juice thing!*

I watched Mia's face closely to catch the slightest glimpse of her wanting to change her mind. There was none. Even though she was scared, she pushed through, and Jase and I let her. We both followed the gurney with tears in our eyes, but she never saw them.

∞

The surgery took almost an hour longer than expected, and just when I was about to rush the doors into the restricted area, Dr. Genecov came out to give us the report. Jase and I hoped, of course, for the same "textbook" report that we had received after the bone graft surgery.

"It was a bit challenging because her mouth is so tiny," he said. "I felt it was too risky to make two separate breaks, so I just made one. But I am very pleased with the result. She is going to do fine."

As soon as he walked away, I cratered. I was relieved that the procedure was a success, but the reality of what Mia had undergone and the daunting course that lay ahead of us suddenly sank in. Once again, we gathered together, and Alan led us all in a prayer of thanksgiving.

Mia was completely out of it for the first few hours after being moved from the recovery room to her intensive care room. She did wake up from time to time to spit blood out of her mouth. The ICU nurse brought in a suction device to help prevent blood from draining down Mia's throat, which caused severe nausea. Keeping the drainage to a minimum was an absolute must, as Mia started vomiting blood every hour or so for the first twelve hours. Jase said that if he had seen that happening in a horror movie, he would have said it was unrealistic. But it was real for Mia, and it was definitely not a pleasant experience. When the nurse saw the concern on our faces, she assured us it was completely normal after a surgery where the jawbone had been cut.

Within the first two hours of being in ICU, Mia was using the suction device herself, with her eyes closed, which definitely impressed the staff. "I have had teenage patients who weren't able to do that," the nurse commented.

Once again, Mrs. LinDee had children from our church and school make decorations for Mia's room, this time creating paper dolls with Scriptures or messages to Mia telling her to "be brave and keep going," a phrase we used to encourage Mia and that we also use today to help bring awareness to all children with clefts. Mrs. LinDee told us that these dolls were a symbol of all of the children standing together with Mia. It was an overwhelming sight! Even though Mia wasn't well enough to even notice them at first, before we left for home she was pointing to certain ones and asking me to read them to her.

At the time of this writing, Mia is still recovering from the distraction operation. After returning home from the hospital, I have had the arduous task of taking a tool that resembles a screwdriver, hooking it onto two screws (one on each side of her upper jaw), and turning it one to three full revolutions each day in order to bring each piece of her jaw forward a little more.

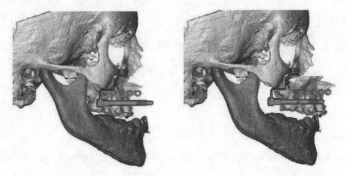

These computer images by Materialise show Mia's actual x-ray (on the left) with Dr. Genecov's Synthes distractor device in place and (on the right) the goal for the repositioned jaw—achieved by manually moving the jaw forward with a tool inserted into the device.

To date, this is by far the hardest procedure and recovery period she has ever had. It has been a painful process for Mia, but again she has demonstrated a massive amount of strength and courage. Even though she has a few more weeks of recovery and is limited in terms of the types of food she enjoys, she never complains of anything other than minor pain. She says she wants to be brave, but asks me sometimes if it is okay to cry.

12
Little Girl, Big Impact

FOR YEARS, our life has been a series of doctor's visits, preparing for surgeries, and looking ahead to the next surgery, knowing it is coming but not allowing the thought of it to rob us of any joy in the present moment. A day will come, though, when either Mia or her doctors decide there will be no more surgeries. Someone will say, "That's it," and surgeries for her cleft lip and palate will be a thing of the past for us. If doctors declare an end to the surgeries, it will be because they have done everything they can possibly do from a medical perspective.

At ICI, the doctors are very much in tune with how patients feel about themselves and diligently try to help them feel as good as possible. The plastic surgeons especially want their work to look the best it can. Once all the surgeries based on medical needs are complete, patients can choose to have additional surgeries for cosmetic purposes if they would like. When that time comes for us, we will let Mia decide what she wants to do. That's a conclusion we came to after sitting in lots of waiting rooms and talking with countless parents of children with cleft lip and palate who are ahead of us on this road.

As much as we must think about Mia's condition, we do not allow it to consume our lives, and she does not allow it to consume her life. She loves her friends, family, school, and church, along with piano lessons, singing, cheerleading, gymnastics, American Girl dolls, pretty dresses, and many other things that girls enjoy.

She approaches each activity with confidence and determination, embracing every moment with a big, bright smile.

Reaching Out

Jase and I decided early in our journey with Mia that we would do our best to try to help other families going through the same situation. When Mia was first diagnosed, we were grateful for the advice we received from other families dealing with cleft conditions, but we also realized that help and support were not abundant. Whenever we became aware of a child with a cleft, we did our best to be available to the family, whether that meant visiting them in the hospital, sharing the names of our doctors, or letting them know what had been helpful or important to us (such as using the tape after the first surgery). We truly felt one reason God allowed us to walk the path He chose for us was to help others, and we wanted to do that in every way possible.

We first started trying to help people about nine months after Mia was born. Through my work at the clinic, I found out about a family who was expecting a baby boy with a cleft lip and palate. I called them and talked to them before his due date, doing my best to help prepare them. When the baby was born, the realities of his condition were completely overwhelming to the family, even though I had told them everything I knew to lessen the shock. They called me right away. That day, I was unable to go to the hospital because Mia was running a fever, so I asked Jase to go see them.

"I *really* don't want to do that," he said.

"Then I need you to come home and watch Mia so I can go."

In the end, it was just easier for Jase to go. Later, when he came home, he described the heart-wrenching scene to me. The baby appeared to have a much more severe condition than Mia did when she was born, and the parents and other family members were beside themselves. Jase recalls walking into the waiting room adjacent to the nursery, where family members could see the baby through a window. The room became awkwardly silent as the large crowd stared at Jase, almost all of them with tears in their eyes. The only thing he could say was "It's going to be okay. I have a daughter with a cleft lip and palate."

He says he felt that the whole family looked to him for support and answers, almost hoping for the magic bullet that would get them out of their situation. He and I both understood how they felt, and he gave them all the encouragement he could— even showing them pictures of Mia before and after both of her surgeries. He did his best to help them feel better and to prepare them for everything they would face in the days and weeks to come. Though it was an emotional experience for him, the family appreciated his efforts, and we are still in touch with them.

In West Monroe, we know of one child in treatment for cleft lip and palate who is about six or seven months ahead of Mia—the Stegalls' son—as well as the boy who is about nine months behind her (the one Jase visited in the hospital when he was born). The Stegall family's advice and encouragement has been so valuable to us, and we have tried to be just as supportive to the family whose child is younger than Mia.

In fact, four families whose children were born with clefts once got together with the rest of the Robertson family for a Christmas party that Jase and I hosted, which was filmed for *Benelli Presents Duck Commander.* Even though we lived within a few miles of one another, our paths mostly crossed in a doctor's office or a hospital in Dallas. But that day, we simply got together for a celebration. Our surprise party guests included one of the surgeons and the anesthesiologist from ICI. It was a happy, memorable time for all of us.

A Way to Help Others

Once *Duck Dynasty* started and Jase and I realized God had given us a significant media platform, we immediately knew that one way we wanted to use it was to raise awareness of cleft lip and palate. By that time, we had seen the impact our faith had on several local families, and we realized that we had been able to help them through some difficult circumstances by sharing the knowledge and experience we had gained and, most of all, by letting them know they were not alone. We felt led to establish a charity—the Mia Moo Fund (www .miamoo.org)—dedicated to helping families going through exactly what we have faced.

The Mia Moo Fund not only provides education about cleft lip and palate but also provides as much practical assistance as possible to children who are undergoing treatment and to their families, such as offering financial assistance for bills not fully covered by insurance and helping parents with travel expenses.

Through this organization, we can support many families we might never have come into contact with, had we not ex-perienced cleft lip and palate firsthand. Because of Mia and her journey, we care deeply about these families and are honored that we are able to help them.

Mia Makes a Difference

I love so many things about being Mia's mom, and one of them is the fact that she cares so much about other people and does all she can to help them. I saw this when she was so excited about her positive influence on her classmate who was willing to wear his headgear to school after she started wearing hers, and I have seen it in countless other ways throughout her life. Numerous people have shared with me that Mia has made a difference in their lives—inspiring them; giving them hope, confidence, and courage because of what they see in her; and strengthening their faith as they observe her childlike faith in action, even when she faces daunting events such as major surgery. I could write pages and pages about Mia's impact on people's lives, but in this book I simply want to share two letters from people who mean a lot to Mia.

In February 2014, Mrs. Rita at OCS asked her fifth grade students to write a letter to someone who really inspired them. Mia's cousins, Bella and Lily, both had this assignment. The two of them never discussed whom they planned to write about in their letters—until the day they handed in the assignment. Bella and Lily had both written their letters to Mia. Here are their letters:

Dear Mia,

You made me the person I am today. You made me stronger. You are the biggest impact in my life. I'm writing this letter to you because in Bible class at school, we were talking about people who made an impact on our lives, and I thought about you. You're so special. God's been with you all your life, and I have too. I have been praying for you every night. I'm so glad we're so close. You're my best friend, and I couldn't live without you. You're my inspiration. We ride bikes together and have so much fun. You're so brave, and I can't wait to see what you do next.

Love,
Bella Rob

Dear Mia,

If I had to pick the bravest person, it would be you. You are an inspiration to a lot of people. You have had a lot of tough surgeries. You are always happy, though. You had to go a long time without Chick-fil-A, which is crazy since nobody can do that but you. I love you, Mia Moo Moo!

Love,

Lily

During their chapel time that day, Bella and Lily read their letters aloud to the rest of the fifth and sixth graders. Mia was in the fourth grade and had a different chapel time, so she wasn't aware that either of them had done this until they told her after school. I happened to be at the school that day, and shortly after the girls read their letters aloud, some of the teachers saw me and, with tears in their eyes, told me what Lily and Bella had done.

Wow! I knew that Jase and I were doing our best to make an impact on people's lives through our own difficulties, but that day I got to see how much of an impact Mia herself was making on the people closest to her. Of course, I ended up crying right alongside those teachers.

Mia Robertson Goes to Washington

A couple of weeks after Mia's bone graft surgery in January 2014, she received a letter from Congressman Trent Franks of Arizona on official United States congressional letterhead. Mia was so excited about the letter that she stood on the fireplace hearth (the living room stage) and proceeded to read it to the entire family. In the letter, Congressman Franks told Mia that he, too, was born with a cleft lip and palate and underwent many surgeries as a child. He told her he understood how she felt and told her not to get discouraged because he recognized how she is helping so many people. He invited her to Washington, DC, to receive an award from Congress for service to her community.

As soon as she had finished reading it to us, she exclaimed, "Can we go?"

Knowing how Jase puts little value on earthly awards and how he likes to travel even less, I responded with a phrase that most parents can understand and appreciate: "We'll see."

Mia immediately ran upstairs and tacked the letter to her bulletin board, full of hope and optimism. How could Jase say no to this?

Oh, she knew her daddy well. He couldn't, and he didn't.

That summer, Mia, Jase, Reed, Cole, and I spent a few days together visiting monuments and historical sites in Washington before meeting Congressman Franks on July 8 in his office on Capitol Hill. Mia's favorite monument was the Lincoln Memorial because she had learned about it in school, so it was cool to see it "for real." It was really crowded there, and people were taking pictures of us while we were trying to read about the monument and take photographs ourselves. Getting Jase out of there took a while because of so many fans wanting pictures—he's very accommodating. That's why it surprised me that this was Mia's favorite site. I'm glad she remembers the impact of the monument and didn't allow the circus of activity from the fans to put a damper on her experience.

Congressman Franks presented Mia with a Certificate of Special Congressional Recognition for "outstanding and invaluable service to the community" at a press conference held at the foot of the Capitol steps. Both he and Mia made speeches that day to numerous cameras and reporters. Hearing my ten-year-old daughter speak about her condition and how she hopes people will look to God to help them get through their own problems was an unbelievably proud moment for me, Jase, and her brothers.

After the press conference, Congressman Franks took us into the House chamber where Congress was voting on a new bill. He took Mia down to the floor, introduced her to some of his colleagues, and let her push his voting button for him. When some of the other members of Congress saw this, they also asked her to push their voting buttons for them.

Of course, Mia wasn't going to push any buttons without quizzing these representatives about what exactly she was voting for. She needed to know what was in the bill before she pushed the buttons. Once she realized she agreed with the bill and saw that some members were voting "no," she commented, "That's just rude." Mia was thrilled with the experience and told us all how she helped make history. Little does she know just how much history she has made and continues to make.

Lessons Learned

People sometimes ask me what I have learned as a result of having a child with medical needs. Having a child with any type of special needs is not a neutral experience; it affects people—often profoundly—one way or another. If I had to summarize how Mia's journey with cleft lip and palate has affected me, I would say it has been a learning experience. I hope and pray some of the lessons I have learned will strengthen and encourage parents who are walking a similar path to the one I have walked as Mia's mom.

I have learned that when people endure suffering, there is a richness that comes to life that they would never experience without it. As I write this book, Reed is nineteen years old and Cole is seventeen, and they have never dealt with the physical challenges and pain Mia has endured. If we did not have Mia in our family, I wonder if we would have lived a good but somewhat shallow life. She has brought so much depth to our lives and to our faith, and she has brought so much meaning to what life is all about.

Mia has taught everyone in our family not to take life so seriously. If anyone has a reason to be sober about certain things, she does. Instead, she is lighthearted, and she trusts God. She does not worry excessively, and she is not a complainer. Of course, she does not always want to do her homework, and she may not like to be encouraged to eat certain foods or to cut short her playtime. But she has never complained about her condition, and that is amazing to me.

I also believe having Mia has made Jase and me better parents to Reed and Cole. Without her, we might have been tempted to take them for granted. Because of the challenges we have faced with Mia, we have always been thankful for the boys' health and well-being, and we have tried to value every moment we have had with them.

One of the lessons I have learned specifically about Mia's cleft is that it is not a problem to be fixed; it is a process to be managed. In the beginning, I simply wanted the surgeons to correct the defects in her lip and palate. It's not that easy. Humans will never be able to recreate what only God can create, no matter how skilled they are. What we can do is manage the challenges we face, get the best care possible, and aim for the best results so a child can have the maximum quality of life as he or she grows older. That's the way Jase and I approach Mia's condition, but we had to learn to see it that way. We could both accurately be described as problem solvers. We like to fix things and move on, so being able to manage a situation with multiple steps over a long period of time instead of trying to fix it all at once was a huge learning curve for us.

Not long after Mia was born, Miss Kay told me something I have always remembered. She said, "God gave her specifically to you because He knows you can handle it. He knows you and Jase will be the best parents she could possibly have."

She went on to ask, "Can you imagine what her life would be like if He had placed her with an immature couple? They just would not be ready for her."

"But I'm not ready either," I said.

Miss Kay responded, "God is saying that you are."

∞

I was reminded of this conversation during the first few days after Mia's distraction surgery. Dr. Genecov had sent us home from the hospital with a special tool for me to use to manually move each piece of Mia's jaw forward one-half of a millimeter each day. He compared it to an orthodontic expander, which I was all too familiar with. However, this was nothing like that expander. With this appliance, I had to tug and pull on Mia's swollen lips and cheeks in order to reach and remove a protective rubber cap from a metal screw on each side of the inside of her mouth, insert the tool onto the screw, and turn it one full turn. It didn't click, snap into place, or give any other sign that it was inserted correctly. The only way I knew that I was completing the task efficiently was when my daughter cried out in pain.

One of the cast members on *Duck Dynasty* is John Godwin, known simply as Godwin. Godwin's wife, Paula, is an RN who is part of my personal support system, so I asked her to be there with me when I first started doing this in case something unexpected happened. Being the wonderful, calm, and skilled soul that she is, not only did she come to our house every day for a week to assist me in this grueling process, she also brought Mia a snow cone to help numb her mouth before each painful episode.

After four days of turning the device, I had a heart-to-heart chat with Paula and Jase in our kitchen, away from Mia's ears. I told them that my biggest fear was showing up at Dr. Genecov's office in three days and hearing him tell me, after looking at her X-rays, that her jaw hadn't moved a bit. I was overwhelmingly unsure whether I had been doing the adjustment correctly.

Is this the expected recovery process? I wondered. *Am I putting my daughter through all this pain for absolutely nothing? How in the world am I supposed to know?!*

Three days later, Mia and I went back to Dallas for X-rays and the follow-up with the doctor. To my relief, the X-rays showed that her jaw was moving and coming together perfectly. Whew!

However, I needed some answers.

"I have a question," I said. "Do you send this tool home with every parent, tell them what to do, and just hope for the best? This is a very meticulous task."

He raised his eyebrows, then looked at me very calmly and said, "No . . . but you're medical."

Surprised at his answer, I answered, "No, I'm not."

"Didn't you work in an ob-gyn clinic for a few years?"

"In the *office*!" I quickly clarified.

"But you *are* a nurse."

"No, I'm not!"

He squared his shoulders, looked me in the eye, and said, "Yes, you are."

Oh, I get it now. Responsible Missy rides in again. You know what I wanted to scream to him? "Wait just a doggone second. Why am I so special? I am sick and tired of being so stinkin' responsible! Why can't I just be like other people I know and be irresponsible and selfish, just this once? It always seems to work out for them. People I know get away with it every day. Why can't I be just like everybody else this one time?"

Then it hit me. Because that's who Mia needs me to be. That's what Miss Kay was talking about when she said that God chose me to be Mia's mom. Nobody else.

Throughout this process, those kinds of thoughts would creep into my mind, so I understand other mothers who also feel that the special needs of their children can be overwhelming at times. When Mia was first born, I didn't want to be as mature as I needed to be, and I didn't want to be as solid and steadfast as I knew I needed to be. There were moments I felt God had been unfair to ask me to deal with the situation He had given us. But God never says life is fair. His Word says He disciplines those He loves (Hebrews 12:6). Every step of our journey with Mia, we have been aware of how much God loves her and how much He loves us.

God Is There

I believe the most important lesson I have learned is the truth of Deuteronomy 31:8: "Do not be afraid or discouraged, for the LORD will personally go ahead of you. He will be with you; *he will neither fail you nor abandon you*" (emphasis added).

At the beginning, I remember having many questions about where God was in the midst of our situation. *What just happened?*

I wondered. *Did God get distracted when Mia was being formed? Did He turn His head for just a second, and this happened when He wasn't paying attention?*

I felt guilty about asking such questions, but I've come to understand that they are normal and understandable when facing a crisis, especially a crisis involving a child. Deep in my heart, I knew God was bigger than all my questions and bigger than the entirety of our situation. By that time, I had known for years that nothing happens that He does not allow. At times I could rest in that knowledge, and at times I thought, *Okay, then why has He allowed this to happen to me?*

I know some people think questioning God represents a lack of faith; I don't see it that way. I think questioning God is okay. In fact, it can be a really good thing to do because asking questions often is the only way to find answers. God Himself says in Jeremiah 29:13, "If you look for me wholeheartedly, you will find me." Had I not allowed myself to wonder where God was at certain points along my journey with Him, I would not have come to the unshakable conviction I now hold—that He will *never* leave us, no matter what.

Because of Mia's condition, our family has met people we never would have encountered otherwise. This also means we have had opportunities to share our faith in ways we might not have had. Early in our experience, I learned to say, "Because we are in this situation, God will be displayed to someone who might have never sought Him otherwise." Boy, has that been true because of Mia!

This is where our faith and trust in God come into play. He knows so much better than we do what is best for us. I knew that in my head at one time, but our experience with Mia has made it a reality in my heart. I've also come to know that God loves my children even more than I do. At times, I wonder if that is even possible. I mean, I think I could stop an oncoming train if it were racing toward Reed, Cole, or Mia. I have that much love for them and that much will to see them protected. I have heard stories of parents who have picked up cars or tractors when their children were trapped underneath; that's how great their love is. As a mom, I understand that. But I also understand that as hard as the concept is to grasp, God loves my children even more than I do. That one thought helps my faith and trust that He is doing what is best, even if I do not fully understand why or how.

Looking back, I now know the answers to questions such as "Where was God when Mia was diagnosed?" I am convinced beyond any shadow of doubt that He was with us. He was right there that day. His eyes were on me; His Spirit was in me, leading me, guiding me, comforting me. Even during the times that I struggled to believe, God was loving Mia and caring for our family in ways I cannot begin to comprehend. Because this is true for us, I can say with absolute conviction and with gratitude that my life is blessed in every way.

More Than I Can Ask or Imagine

When Mia was first diagnosed, one of the major concerns we had was her speech. Being from a musical family, I was highly concerned about my daughter being able to carry on the talents that were passed down to my boys and me from my mom's side of the family. My mom has a master's degree in vocal music and taught me everything I know about vocal performance. I, in turn, have passed my knowledge down to Reed and Cole over the years and planned to do this with our baby girl. But when Mia was born, I realized that this dream of mine might be much harder, if not impossible, for her. However, she not only learned to speak clearly; she also learned to sing beautifully. Her first public debut was singing "God Bless America" on a Duck Commander video when she was only three years old.

Paul wrote in Ephesians 3:20-21, "Now to him who is able to do immeasurably more than all we ask or imagine, according to his power that is at work within us, to him be glory in the church and in Christ Jesus throughout all generations, for ever and ever! Amen" (NIV). Amen to that!

∞

A few months before her bone graft surgery, Mia asked if she could go with me to my next speaking engagement and talk about her cleft. We sat down and wrote a speech together— becoming a dynamic dual package for this event and others that followed. After I spoke, I introduced Mia. She gave her speech and sang "This Little Light of Mine"—the Addison Road version, reminding everyone that "there's a little flame inside us all" and how important it is to let it shine, no matter what. Every time she has given this speech, she receives a standing ovation, with lots of whooping and hollering and quite a few tears brushed away from faces in the audience.

Mia gave a speech on March 7, 2015, just three weeks before her distraction surgery. I've included it here in the hope that you, the reader, will hear Mia's voice and share in her courage, which she so willingly displays in order to encourage others to make the decision to be brave and keep going.

This ability for Mia and our family to use our challenges to benefit others is just one more reason I consider myself blessed.

My name is Mia Elaine Robertson, and I was born on
September 12, 2003. The doctor wanted to deliver me
on 9/11, but my mom asked her to wait until the next
day. She said I was going to have a few problems
to overcome in life already, and she didn't want my
birthday to add to that. You see, I was born with a
cleft lip and cleft palate. My mom and dad knew about
it ahead of time because they saw it on an ultrasound,
so they were able to find me the best doctors in all of
America before I was even born. The doctors work
in Dallas.

I've had five surgeries so far. My last one was on
January 3, 2014. It was a biggie. They took bone from
my hip and put it in my top jaw. I had to drink all my
food for three months. I did okay with this, but I really
missed Chick-fil-A! I have another surgery in a few
weeks on March 27, 2015.

When I think about my cleft, sometimes I feel like
people laugh at me. But I think like my dad did when he
got kicked out of the Trump Hotel;[4] I just need to laugh
it off. I'm not the type of person who sits around
and thinks about it all the time. I'm too busy with
other stuff, like school, piano, cheerleading, music, and
playing with my cousins.

I tell you this about myself because I believe that
God has called me for a special purpose, just like He
did Moses in Exodus. Moses couldn't believe that God,
the Creator of the entire universe, would pick him to
do such a big job for His people. He made excuses to
God about his speaking ability in Exodus 4:10-12:[5]

[Moses said,] "Master, please, I don't talk well. I've never been good with words, neither before nor after you spoke to me. I stutter and stammer."

GOD said, "And who do you think made the human mouth? And who makes some mute, some deaf, some sighted, some blind? Isn't it I, GOD? So, get going. I'll be right there with you—with your mouth! I'll be right there to teach you what to say."

Just like He called Moses, God has called me to use my mouth to share the message of Jesus with thousands of people.

I hope I can grow up spreading the love of Jesus to lots of people so they can go to heaven with us. My favorite verse is Psalm 46:10, which says, "Be still, and know that I am God!" I like this verse because whenever I feel sad or have struggles, I know that God is bigger than all of that. And He is bigger than any of your struggles too. And don't forget that.

Thank you.

—Mia Robertson (age 11)

Acknowledgments

TO JASE—This has been a tough road at times, and I could not have had the strength to press on through each valley if it weren't for your consistency, dedication, and humor. I thank God for the mountaintop experiences with you, too, and there have been many! Thank you for keeping me laughing, encouraging me to have a positive spirit, and most of all, for keeping our little family always pointing heavenward.

To Mia—Your confidence in yourself and in God to always take care of you makes my jaw drop at times. You are my inspiration to get through any trial that may come my way. Because of your undeniable character, there is no doubt that God will continue to use you in a big way for Him. Keep letting your light shine. I can't wait to see what He does next!

To Jan, Bonne, Jillian, Sharon, and all the folks at Tyndale House Publishers—Thank you for partnering with me in this endeavor. I pray that God will use all of us through this book to encourage as many brokenhearted and discouraged people to put their faith in God and to trust that He can get them through any heartache.

To Beth Clark—Once again, you have done an amazing job

in putting my thoughts, feelings, outbursts, joys, and frustrations on paper in such an inspiring way. Thank you for bearing with all my nitpickiness (is that a word?) and respecting my desires for my own words to be heard.

Endnotes

1. Alan and Lisa's story can be found in their book with Beth Clark, *A New Season: A Robertson Family Love Story of Brokenness and Redemption* (New York: Howard Books, 2015).
2. "Cleft Lip and Cleft Palate," the website of Mayo Clinic, Diseases and Conditions, last modified January 27, 2015, http://www.mayoclinic .org/diseases-conditions/cleft-palate/basics/definition/CON-20024619.
3. "A cleft lip is a physical split or separation of the two sides of the upper lip and appears as a narrow opening or gap in the skin of the upper lip. This separation often extends beyond the base of the nose and includes the bones of the upper jaw and/or upper gum. A cleft palate is a split or opening in the roof of the mouth. A cleft palate can involve the hard palate (the bony front portion of the roof of the mouth), and/or the soft palate (the soft back portion of the roof of the mouth)." From "Cleft Lip and Cleft Palate," *WebMD*, last reviewed January 22, 2015, http://www.webmd. com/oral-health/guide/cleft-lip-cleft-palate.
4. When the Robertsons were in New York City to promote the season four premiere of *Duck Dynasty*, they were staying at the Trump International Hotel. The group decided to go to a Broadway musical, and while everyone was gathering in the lobby, Jase asked the doorman where the nearest restroom was. The doorman gave him directions to the hotel restaurant. There, a staff person offered his assistance. Not knowing who Jase was (and possibly thinking he was a street person), the man courteously walked Jase out of the hotel and wished him a nice day. Jase laughed it off, jokingly labeling the incident "facial profiling." For the complete story, see Jase Robertson with Mark Schlabach, *Good Call: Reflections on Faith, Family, and Fowl* (Nashville: Howard Books, 2014), 178–179.
5. Exodus 4:10-12 taken from *The Message*.

Discussion Guide

1. Missy shares some of the differences between her and Jase's lifestyles growing up. Where Missy's home was more structured, Jase's was more laid-back. What are the differences between your upbringing and the upbringing of your spouse or significant other? Do you find those differences still challenge your relationship now? In what ways?

2. Missy and Jase made a deal in their marriage: Jase could hunt every day of duck season as long as their children went to the Christian school Missy had attended growing up. What are some agreements that you have made with your significant other? Do you still hold them in place today?

3. Upon hearing about and understanding the extreme pain that would be involved in childbirth, a young Missy declared to her parents that she would NOT be having children. Those feelings changed as she became a wife. What were some declarations that you made as a child that have since changed now that you're an adult? What assisted in changing your mind?

4. When Missy discovered that her third pregnancy was a tubal pregnancy and needed to be terminated, she was understandably upset and grieved by the news. The two surgeries and extensive recovery period were very hard on her. The simple help that the Robertson family received during that time (cleaning up the house, being given meals, having childcare), helped alleviate some stress and worry. How have you been the recipient of someone else's generosity? How did that little act of kindness help you? What are some ways that you can lend a hand to someone else?

5. We all have different ways of handling situations. After learning of Mia's cleft lip (and potential cleft palate) while pregnant, Missy went into "fix it" mode and learned everything she could about her daughter's condition. She talked to medical personnel and made a plan of attack. How do you handle challenging situations? Give an example.

6. After a long, exhausting day of meeting with all of Mia's doctors at the International Craniofacial Institute just seventeen days after Mia's birth, Missy broke down that evening at the thought of Mia's long medical journey ahead. Jase simply did not want to talk about it and went right to sleep. But the next day, he came up with a plan that gave responsibilities to their young boys that helped the entire family. How do you cope or release your emotions in difficult situations? Does talking help, or do you prefer to be alone? Give an example.

7. One adjustment Missy needed to make regarding Mia's condition was working her way out of denial mode and embracing the truth of their reality. Can you recall a time

when you needed to go through different stages of grief over a situation that you or your family was involved in? What helped you decide to keep going and not give up?

8. After Missy and Jase learned that their home was robbed, friends and family members surrounded them with generosity of simple gifts and prayer. When has someone "rescued" you with unexpected thoughtfulness? How has that simple gesture changed you?

9. Through many surgeries, Mia's friends, schoolmates, and cousins gathered alongside her and encouraged her with cards, support, and kindness. When have you witnessed children blessing others with encouragement and grace?

10. Even though Mia was born with special needs, her life has been rich with blessings. Think of a difficult circumstance in which you saw God work so many wondrous things through it. Maybe it's been something in your own life. Maybe you can't quite see the blessings yet. Hang in there. With God, all things are possible. Romans 8:31 says, "What, then, shall we say in response to these things? If God is for us, who can be against us?" (NIV)

About the Authors

MISSY ROBERTSON has learned to live life in the spotlight as she plays an important part in her family's record-breaking reality television series, *Duck Dynasty*. Despite the increased publicity focused on her family, their company, and their personal lives, she has managed to become a strong voice for morality and virtue, both locally and globally.

Missy married Jase Robertson when she was nineteen and is now a devoted mother of three children—Reed, Cole, and Mia—who strives to have a strong, happy, and loving family. She has contributed heavily to the Robertson family business, Duck Commander, and has been an integral part of the success that the family and company have seen in recent years.

Missy is always the first to recognize the hand of God in her life, as she continually sets a prime example of humility and consistent faith in her public and personal life. In gratitude for her many blessings, she spends a large amount of her time volunteering as a way to give back to her community. For the last six summers, she has been the crafts director at Camp Ch-Yo-Ca, a local Christian youth camp where both she and Jase spent many summers as kids. In addition, she is heavily involved in missionary work, both domestically and internationally.

Missy is featured on the platinum-selling album, *Duck the Halls: A Robertson Family Christmas*, released in 2013. In early 2014, Missy coauthored *The Women of Duck Commander* with Miss Kay and her sisters-in-law, in which they shared never-before-told stories about the Robertson family and how their reliance on God has enabled them to persevere through life's unforeseen challenges, heartaches, and strife.

Missy helps design modest and stylish apparel for her clothing line, Missy Robertson by Southern Fashion House, and has recently launched *Laminin*, a jewelry line that is made in her hometown of West Monroe, Louisiana. On her website, www .missyrobertson.com, Missy keeps her fans up-to-date on her latest clothing and jewelry lines and offers a devotional page to help encourage people to pursue a personal relationship with God.

Missy is also known for her hard work supporting the Mia Moo Fund, an organization inspired by their family's personal journey and launched in 2014 to raise awareness and funds toward research, treatments, and causes of cleft lip and palate.

Beth Clark is a writer and consultant based in Franklin, Tennessee. She has a passion for great stories and has written numerous *New York Times* bestselling books, including *Kisses from Katie* with Katie Davis and *The Women of Duck Commander* with Kay, Korie, Missy, Jessica, and Lisa Robertson.

Notes

MIA MOO

because every kid deserves a smile

THE MIA MOO FUND is a nonprofit organization created by Jase, Missy, and Mia Robertson. The Mia Moo Fund is dedicated to raising awareness and funds toward the management, treatments, and surgical procedures for domestic children affected by cleft lip and palate. We at the Mia Moo Fund want to inform and inspire families and improve the quality of life for children born with cleft lip and palate. Our overall desire is that these children learn that they have a wonderful and unique purpose in life that only they can fulfill.

To learn more and donate, please visit MiaMoo.org.

Bring *BLESSED, BLESSED . . . BLESSED* to your community!

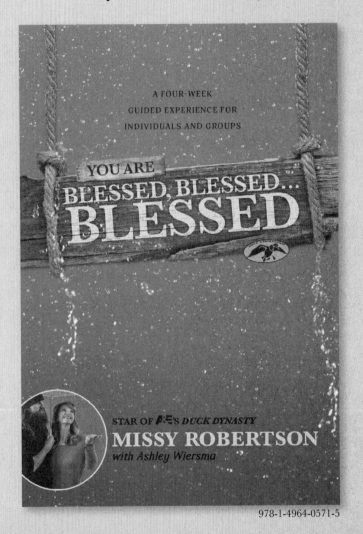

A FOUR-WEEK
GUIDED EXPERIENCE FOR
INDIVIDUALS AND GROUPS

YOU ARE
BLESSED, BLESSED...
BLESSED

STAR OF A+E's *DUCK DYNASTY*
MISSY ROBERTSON
with *Ashley Wiersma*

978-1-4964-0571-5